THE FRIGATE
DIANA

**Anatomy
of the
Ship**

THE FRIGATE
DIANA

David White

Naval
Institute
Press

Frontispiece
1. The starboard quarter of NMM model
number 1794–2 showing the decoration of
the stern and quarter galleries to advantage.
Notice also the fine run aft to the round tuck
stern.

First published in Great Britain 1987 by
Conway Maritime Press Ltd
24 Bride Lane, Fleet Street,
London EC4Y 8DR

Published and distributed in the United
States of America and Canada by the
Naval Institute Press, Annapolis,
Maryland 21402.

Library of Congress Catalog Card No.
87–62394

ISBN 0–87021–202–8

Contents

Introduction

Wartime inevitably provides a great boost for warship design and construction; not only does it provide greater incentive but equally importantly it also provides the necessary finance. It is therefore not surprising to find that on 6 November 1778, just five months after the entry of France into the War of American Independence, the Board of Admiralty had arrived at the stage where it was able to establish one of the most significant milestones in the history of the British sailing frigate. On that day the Board ordered two new ships to be built, one at Deptford Dockyard and one at Woolwich Dockyard. These ships were the first two frigates to be ordered with a main armament of 18-pounder guns, 12-pounders having been the largest guns carried until then.

When *Flora* was launched at Deptford eighteen months later she was the first 36-gun ship to have been built for the Navy for twenty-two years. A month later *Minerva* was launched at Woolwich and made history by becoming the first British 38-gun ship to be built. She was followed by a sister ship *Arethusa* in 1781 and by two further sisters *Phaeton* and *Thetis*, with slightly modified hulls, in 1782.

In the eighteenth century there were two Surveyors of the Navy at any one time and it was common practice for each one to produce a design to the same specification when new ships were contemplated. The new 38-gun ships were no exception. The *Minerva*, designed by Edward Hunt, was followed into the water nine months later by *Latona*, to the design of Sir John Williams. The latter was presumably the less successful of the two designs as it was not repeated.

Although the *Minerva*s showed themselves to be good ships they suffered from one serious fault: they were too small for their armament. The problem was not one of weight, as they had been given a new lighter 8-foot 18-pounder gun, instead of the standard 9-foot one. It was one of space: the guns were too close together. The design was modified by reducing the number of guns on the upper deck by two, with a consequent increase in the space between the remainder of some 8 or 9 inches. In January 1783, just as the War of American Independence ended, a new draught to build this 36-gun version was sent to Messrs Hilhouse of Bristol, who had built *Arethusa* two years before. Although this ship, *Melampus*, was completed two years later no further frigates were to be ordered until the advent of the Revolutionary War in 1793.

This new war started on 1 February and on the 14th of the same month the Admiralty ordered the Navy Board to prepare draughts for a proposed new class of six 38-gun ships, to be built in merchant yards. Although frigate building had been at a standstill for almost a decade the Navy Board had obviously been keeping up to date with its design work, for the new draught was delivered to the Admiralty only eight days later. Their Lordships approved it on 2 March and on the same day the Navy Board produced a further, slightly modified draught endorsed 'for building'. Copies of this were sent to the builders for *Artois* and *Apollo* on 22 March, *Diamond* and *Diana* on 28 March and *Seahorse* and *Janus* on 1 April. Contracts must have been negotiated whilst the copies of the draught were being made as it is on record that work on *Diana* commenced in March.

The new ships, with a lower deck length of 146 feet, were 5 feet longer than the *Minerva*s, giving them an increase in space between the guns of just under 5 inches. Once the ships got into service, however, it soon became apparent that this increase was quite inadequate and so the Admiralty experimented with a series of one-off ships in the hope of arriving at a suitable design. These were *Naiad* (147ft), *Hydra* (148ft 2in), *Boadicea* (148ft 6in) together with *Amazon*, *Hussar* and *Active* (150ft); *Amazon* and *Hussar* were sister ships and *Active* was an enlarged *Artois*. None of these designs was perpetuated and in the end the *Leda*, based on the lines of the French ship *Hebe* captured in 1782, was chosen as the model for the standard 38-gun frigate. The *Leda* class ultimately became the largest class of sailing frigates ever built for the Royal Navy. No less than forty-seven were built between 1800 and 1830, in four different versions.

Concurrently with these experimental ships a further three *Artois* class ships were built. The first two were *Clyde* and *Tamer*, both built in Chatham Dockyard, and differing from their more conventional sisters in that they were largely built of fir and had square tuck sterns. The last ship of the class, *Ethalion*, was virtually identical to the first six. Brief details of the class are given in Table 1.

TABLE 1: **ARTOIS CLASS**

Name	Launched	Builder	Disposal	
Artois	3 Jan 1794	Wells, Rotherhithe	Wrecked	31 July 1797
Diana	3 Mar 1794	Randall, Rotherhithe	Sold	7 Mar 1815
Diamond	17 Mar 1794	Barnard, Deptford	Broken up	June 1812
Apollo	18 Mar 1794	Perry, Blackwall	Wrecked	7 Jan 1799
Jason	3 Apr 1794	Dudman, Deptford	Wrecked	13 Aug 1798
Seahorse	11 June 1794	Stalkartt, Rotherhithe	Broken up	July 1819
Clyde	26 Mar 1796	Chatham dockyard	Sold	Aug 1814
Tamer	26 Mar 1796	Chatham dockyard	Broken up	Jan 1810
Ethalion	14 Mar 1797	Graham, Harwich	Wrecked	19 Dec 1799

DESIGN

The two Surveyors of the Navy in 1793 were Sir William Rule and Sir John Henslow, the latter being responsible for the design of *Diana* and her sisters.

There was nothing revolutionary about the lines of the ships. They used a conventional three-sweep midship section with variable length floor sweep radii based on a diagonal. Undoubtedly the modified *Minerva* lines that were used for *Phaeton* and *Thetis* were taken as a basis for the new class, as below the lower height of breadth the midships sections are almost identical. By lowering the lower height of breadth approximately 6 inches amidships and 18 inches at the extremities, Sir John made very little difference to the waterline amidships

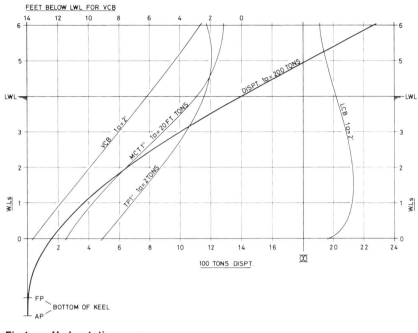

FEET BELOW LWL FOR VCB

100 TONS DISPT.

Fig 1	**Hydrostatic curves**
LWL	Load waterline
LCB	Longitudinal centre of buoyancy
VCB	Vertical centre of buoyancy
MCT1″	Moment to change trim one inch
TP1″	Tons per inch immersion

TABLE 3: **SECONDARY DIMENSIONS**

Lengths	ft	in
From fore side of the taffarel at the height of the fife rail to fore side of the figure	173	9
From fore side of the stem to fore side of the knee of the head	13	4
From after side of the wing transom to after side of the stern timber at the angle of the lower counter on the middle line	5	7
From after side of the wing transom to after side of the stern timber at the angle of the second counter on the middle line	7	6½
Moulded breadths		
Amidships	38	6
At the height of breadth at the aftermost part of the counter	25	0
At the toptimber line amidships	35	2
At the toptimber line aft	20	0
Heights above the upper side of the keel		
Cutting down line amidships	1	7½
Lower deck – upper side of the plank on the middle line at the after side of the stem	17	0
– at the fore side of the rabbet of the stern post	18	5
Upper side of the wing transom at the stern post	22	1
Angle of the lower counter on the middle line	26	1
Lower height of breadth amidships	16	8½
Upper height of breadth amidships	19	1½
Toptimber line – at the stem	29	8
– amidships	27	11
– at the stern timber	32	8
Height between decks on the middle line		
From upper side of orlop beams to lower side of lower deck plank	5	1
From upper side of after platform to lower side of lower deck plank	6	0
From upper side of fore platform to lower side of lower deck plank	5	3
From plank of the lower deck to upper side of upper deck beams	6	4
From plank of the upper deck to upper side of quarterdeck beams – forward	6	6
– aft	7	0
From plank of the upper deck to upper side of forecastle beams	6	6
From plank of the upper deck to gunwale	6	9
From plank of the upper deck to lower port sills	2	1

TABLE 2: **BASIC DIMENSIONS**

	As designed		As built	
	ft	in	ft	in
Length on lower deck	146	0	146	3
Length of keel for tonnage	121	7⅛	121	8½
Breadth extreme	39	0	39	3½
Depth in hold	13	9	13	9
Burthen in tons	983⁷⁰⁄₉₄		999⁴³⁄₉₄	

but produced a fuller waterline fore and aft, probably in order to reduce pitching. Shortening the lower breadth sweeps produced a slightly finer hull throughout and altering the floor sweeps gave a moderately sharper entry and a finer run aft. Combined with the increase in length these alterations should have resulted in a better performance. The hollow floors which were one of the features which distinguished the second pair of *Minerva*s from the first pair were retained in a less exaggerated form.

As already mentioned the lower height of breadth admidships was lowered about 6 inches. At the same time the upper height of breadth was raised and the upper breadth sweeps were lengthened. This reduced tumblehome and increased the width of the decks. The basic design dimensions are given in Table 2, which also gives the dimensions as built for comparison. Secondary design dimensions can be found in Table 3.

CONSTRUCTION

Diana was built by Randall and Brent of Rotherhithe. This company had three yards on the Thames, totalling between them seven building ships, two double docks and one single dock. They were situated one on either side of the Greenland Dock and one at Cuckold's Point on the site of what is now Nelson Dock. It is not known at which of these yards *Diana* was built.

The company was one of the biggest merchant builders in the country and had constructed many ships for the Royal Navy. The first ship known to have been built by them was the 28-gun frigate *Tartar*, launched at Cuckold's Point in April 1756. She was also the first frigate to be built in a merchant yard, having been launched some six weeks before her sister ship *Lowestoffe*, even although the latter had been ordered three weeks before her. These two ships had the added distinction of being the first ones to have been designed as frigates, as opposed to being designed as 24-gun ships and later re-armed as 28s.

Randall and Brent's contract, in line with the practice of the day, was to supply the completed hull only, at a rate of £14 per ton. The tonnage figure used to arrive at the total value was calculated from the design dimensions; the contract was quite emphatic about this. Most ships exceeded their designed dimensions, and consequently their designed tonnage. Increase in beam due to the frames falling outwards during building was the commonest error and as the tonnage figures were proportional to the square of the beam it was the most significant one also. *Diana*'s designed tonnage was 983 ⁷⁰⁄₉₄ giving a value of

£13,772. She exceeded her designed dimensions by 3 inches in length and 3½ inches in breadth, increasing her tonnage to 999 $^{43}/_{94}$. Using this figure to calculate her value it would have increased payment by £80. However, had the frames been allowed to fall out another 2½ inches increasing the beam by a total of 6 inches – a figure that was by no means uncommon – then the tonnage would have risen to 1011 $^{11}/_{94}$ and the value on this basis to £14,155.

Minor adjustments were made to the basic amount. Additions were made for items supplied or jobs done which were not specified in the original contract. Deductions were made for items 'found by His Majesty', amongst which were such things as mixt metal or copper underwater fittings. The final amount received by the contractors was £13,788.

The contract laid down the scantlings of every major timber in the ship. The types of timber, elm for the keel, oak for the frames and so on, were often specified for specific items and the following paragraph covered the rest:

That all the Timber and Plank shall be of the Growth of England, except the Plank of the Bottom under the light Draught of Water, which may be East Country Plank, provided it be good white Crown Plank, otherwise to be English Plank. All the Knees, Standards, Riders, Crutches, and Breast Hooks to have so full a faying of Spine against the respective Beams, Sides, Decks, Ceilings &c that the Bolts for fastening of each may not be naked when the Sap rots away, as has too frequently appeared, to the evident weakening of Ships formerly built in Merchants Yards, and has proved the principal Means of their too soon Decay; and also the whole Frame to be well grown, square edged, free from Sap, Shakes, and Defects; and that all the Plank of the Bottom, Sides, and Decks, shall be dry and well seasoned before it is wrought; and that all the Prussia Deals for the Decks, &c be good, yellow Wood, free from Sap, Shakes or Defects, and that no Sap shall be wrought in the Edges of them.

In addition to specifying the timber scantlings the contract also dealt with ironwork of all types; use of iron knees, size and numbers of bolts, eyebolts, swivels, ringbolts etc. In general it stated that 'All the Iron Work shall be wrought out of the best sort of Orgrounds Iron, not burnt, or hurt in working; all the Bolts to be clenched or belayed, as shall be directed; those to the Iron Knees and Standards to be drove through them into the Transoms, Beams, or Timbers, and all clenched on Rings let into the Wood.'

Construction followed the normal pattern for the period and the outboard appearance was typical of ships in the first part of the last decade of the eighteenth century, a period regarded by many as being the zenith of the development of the sailing warship. The garish top-heavy sterns of the late seventeenth and early eighteenth centuries had long since disappeared, while the open rails of the quarterdeck, although berthed up, still retained their elegant serpentine curves at the forward end, a feature they were soon to lose. In fact only the first six ships of the class had this feature; the last three were built with ugly square-cut bulwarks on the quarterdeck.

With the exception of a few of the very earliest ships all frigates had a shapely round bow, culminating in a lightly built head with a full-length figure, as opposed to the ugly beakhead bulkhead of the larger ships. *Diana* and her first five sisters were amongst the last ships, other than First Rates, to have a full-length figure, as the Admiralty issued an order in 1796 abolishing the fitting of new ones in Second Rates and below. The last three ships of the class were fitted with the scroll head that the Admiralty decreed should replace the figure. Such was the outcry against this austerity, however, that the Admiralty partly relented a few years later and allowed ships to have a bust instead – but the full-length figure for frigates had unfortunately gone forever.

Diana and all her sisters retained the open timberheaded forecastle of their predecessors which was to be replaced a few years later by the more utilitarian, but less aesthetically pleasing, built-up square bulwarks of the nineteenth century. They also had a feature in common with all of Sir John Henslow's ships, which no other frigates had, in that they had four head timbers instead of the more usual three.

The ship's bottom was payed with 'Tar boiled to a strong resistance, or as shall be directed' and the sides were painted from the wales upwards with 'three good Coats of Paint, the last Coat to be of a yellow cast.' The great cabin, steerage, all the cabins, rails, stanchions, ladders, gratings, gangways, bulkheads, capstans, upper deck beams and knees were also given three coats of paint 'and all Work in Wake of them, and without Board for finishing and compleating the Hull of the said Ship, shall be done in a workmanlike Manner, equal in all Respects to those of His Majesty's Ships of the like Quality in the King's Yards.'

Eleven months after building was started, on 3 March 1794, *Diana* was launched and towed the short distance downstream to the Royal Dockyard at Deptford where she was to be fitted out. She was docked the next day, her bottom was coppered, and she returned to the water on 13 March. Her progress from then onwards can be summarised by extracts from the Master's log, with comments in brackets.

April 14	Lt England commissioned the ship [he was the first lieutenant; the captain, Johnathon Faulknor, had yet to join]
22	Riggers began by contract
May 3	Riggers finished [13 days inclusive. They worked a seven-day week]
15	Blacked the yards. Received anchors
25	Received cables
29	Received sails. Painters onboard
June 7	Ran down the river at midnight to Gravesend
10	Received Gunner's stores and carronades
11	Received guns
12	Unmoored and ran for the Nore

The cost of the ship's masts and yards was £2675 and that of her rigging and stores a further £5528. An approximate breakdown of the latter figure can be obtained by taking average proportionate figures obtained from similar ships of the same period. These are:

	%	£
Rigging	26	1437
Sails	14	774
Anchors	8	442
Cables	14	774
Boatswain's stores	13	719
Carpenter's stores	13	1382

This brings the cost of building and fitting the ship for sea to £21,991 plus the cost of supplying the underwater copper fittings. To this must be added at least another £1000 for guns and the Gunner's stores, bringing the total cost to over £23,000.

RIGGING

Like all other frigates *Diana* was ship rigged. That is to say that she had three masts, all of which were square rigged. In 1794, when she was built, frigates' masts were composed of three parts: a lower mast, a topmast and a topgallant mast. Each of these components carried a yard at right angles to it and with the exception of the mizen mast each yard carried a sail. The yard on the mizen (lower) mast was known as the crossjack. Those on the main and fore (lower) masts were the main and fore yards respectively, their sails being the main sail, or main course, and the fore sail, or fore course. The yards on the topmasts were named after their sails, not after the masts, being the mizen, main and fore topsail yards. Those on the topgallant masts were known simply as the mizen, main and fore topgallant yards and carried mizen, main and fore topgallant sails.

All ships were supplied with topgallant masts of two or sometimes three lengths. The longest of these, the long pole head topgallant mast, was only rigged in fair weather and was long enough to carry an additional sail above the topgallant. Commonly called the royal, this sail was actually the topgallant royal and should not be confused with the true royal which was carried on a separate royal mast. Frigates in 1794 were not fitted with royal masts.

Topgallant royals were set flying: that is to say that the only running rigging that they had was a halliard. There were no braces or sheets, the clues of the sails being seized to the topgallant yardarms. True royals, on their own masts, were fully rigged in the same way that the topgallants were.

Diana, when first rigged, carried one other square sail. This was the spritsail, which was carried on a yard slung under the bowsprit. Added to the courses, topsails, topgallants and topgallant royals this brought the total number of square sails to twelve. The courses had two reef bands and the mizen topsail three but the main and fore topsails would have had the four bands laid down by the Admiralty Order of 4 November 1788.

The main and fore courses, topsails and topgallants could be extended by means of studding sails on either side. Studding sails were never fitted on the mizen. The mizen however carried a large fore and aft sail, known as a driver, spread between a gaff and a boom and in the words of the authorising Admiralty Order 'in the form of a brig's mainsail'. A mizen staysail, mizen topmast staysail and a mizen topgallant staysail were carried between the mizen and main masts, although in practice the last named was seldom used. Between the main and foremasts the staysails carried were the main staysail, main topmast staysail, middle staysail and main topgallant staysail, whilst ahead of the foremast were the fore staysail, fore topmast staysail and jib. Storm main and fore staysails were also provided so that a full suit of sails, when first commissioned, consisted of twelve square sails, twelve studding sails and thirteen fore and aft sails; a total of thirty-seven, not including spares.

This total was not to last for long, however. On 18 August 1794 a Navy Board warrant authorised the introduction of a flying jib and its associated flying jibboom. Further additions to the sail plan followed, together with alterations to the rigging – some official, some not. In September the logs mention a spanker. As the names spanker and driver were both used indiscriminately when referring to the driver it is difficult to establish when the loose-footed spanker was actually acquired. The Master's log suggests that it had been in existence from the very beginning. In June 1795 it records the use of a spritsail topsail yard as a replacement for a damaged main topgallant yard, but there is no mention of actually using a spritsail topsail at this period. In January 1796 *Diana*'s fore mast was moved 4 inches aft, possibly as a counter to the flying jib. Strangely, two of her sisters, *Jason* and *Diamond*, had their fore masts moved forward 6¼ inches the following year, the year that the Admiralty authorised the issue of main trysails and gaffs.

The first mention of royal masts being fitted that has been found is dated 13 February 1808. They must have existed before that, however, because in August 1806 *Diana* was setting not only royals but skyscrapers, which upsets the commonly held view that they were introdudced by the Americans in the War of 1812. (Skyscrapers were set flying above royals, on the royal mast, just as the topgallant royals had been set flying above topgallants when the ship first commissioned.) At the same time she also set a spritsail topsail, obsolete by then, together with two sails which officially did not exist: a gaff topsail and a crossjack, both of which are associated with the clipper sail era rather than with the Napoleonic Wars. There is also mention of an inner jib in 1806 but this may well have been a change of name for the fore topmast staysail, rather than being an additional sail.

Main lower studding sails had officially been abolished by an Admiralty Order in 1801. By 1807 royal studding sails and an upper main staysail were being carried, bringing *Diana*'s unofficial outfit to at least forty-nine, plus spares.

The mast and spar dimensions of the ship, as first fitted, are listed in Tables 4 and 5. Table 6 lists the probable belaying points at the same time.

ARMAMENT

The standard main armament of a 38-gun frigate consisted of twenty-eight 18-pounder carriage guns on one deck, the upper deck. *Diana* was no exception to this and she carried these guns throughout her career. They were mounted on standard carriages and the only way that they differed from the usual 18-pounder gun of the period was that, in common with the guns carried by all the 38-gun ships of the period, they were only 8 feet long. The reason why the 38-gun ships carried 8-foot guns when the standard 18-pounder was 9 feet long is straightforward. It was a matter of weight. The early 38s were virtually no bigger than contemporary 36s; in fact the 36-gun *Melampus* was actually a sister ship of the first 38s, the *Minerva*s. *Melampus* was able to carry twenty-six 9-foot guns satisfactorily; *Minerva* was only able to carry two extra guns because the weight of twenty-eight short guns was virtually the same as the weight of twenty-six long ones.

The original design for *Diana* and her sisters called for eight 9-pounder carriage guns on the quarterdeck, with a further two on the forecastle. The quarterdeck guns were to be 7 feet long; the forecastle ones, being chase guns, 6 inches longer to give them extra range. These were standard guns, on standard carriages and all the ships of the class carried them when first built.

The carronade armament was more complex. Although these close-range weapons had been established in the Navy as early as 1779 both the 'proposed' and the 'for building' draughts for the *Artois* class made no provision for them. The Navy Board copy of the contract for the class, which is on a standard printed form, has the sizes of the carronade ports overwritten on it and yet still specifies details of the stocks for the swivel guns that the carronades superseded.

An Admiralty Order of 25 November 1782 specified 24-pounder carronades for 38-gun ships in lieu of 18-pounders, but there is no evidence to show that this was ever put into effect. The fact that hostilities ended two months later probably accounts for this. When the Revolutionary War broke out in 1793 *Minerva* was ordered to fit 18-pounders and this was the weight of metal fitted to the ships of the *Artois* class when first built. They carried four carronades on the quarterdeck and two on the forecastle.

TABLE 4: **MAST DIMENSIONS**

Mast	Overall		Head		Long pole head		Proper pole head		Stump pole head		Diam
	ft	in	ft	in	ft	in	ft	in	ft	in	in
Main	92	6	12	10							27¾
Main topmast	55	6	6	2							16½
Main topgallant	27	9			16	8	10	9½	2	8½	9¼
Fore	82	3	11	5							24⅝
Fore topmast	49	4	5	5¾							16½
Fore topgallant	24	8			14	10	9	7	2	5	8¼
Mizen	79	3½	8	9¾							18½
Mizen topmast	41	7½	4	0½							11½
Mizen topgallant	20	9¾			12	6½	8	1	2	0	7
Bowsprit	55	6									27¾
Jibboom	39	7½									11½

TABLE 5: **SPAR DIMENSIONS**

Spar	Length		Diam
	ft	in	in
Main yard	82	3	19¼
Main topsail yard	58	9	12¼
Main topgallant yard	35	3	7
Main royal yard	29	5	6⅛
Fore yard	72	0	16¾
Fore topsail yard	51	5	10¾
Fore topgallant yard	30	10	6¼
Fore royal yard	25	9	5⅜
Crossjack	51	5	10¾
Mizen topsail yard	39	2	8¼
Mizen topgallant yard	23	6	4¾
Mizen royal yard	19	7	4⅛
Spritsail yard	51	5	10¾
Driver boom	58	9	10¾
Driver gaff	36	9	10¾
Main lower studding sail boom	45	8	9¼
Main topmast studding sail boom	29	4½	8¼
Main topgallant studding sail boom	17	7½	6
Fore lower studding sail boom	45	8	9¼
Fore topmast studding sail boom	36	0	7¼
Fore topgallant studding sail	25	9	5¼
Main lower studding sail yard	26	1	5¼
Main topmast studding sail yard	16	9½	4¼
Main topgallant studding sail yard	10	8½	3
Fore lower studding sail yard	45	8	9¼
Fore topmast studding sail yard	20	7	4¼
Fore topgallant studding sail yard	14	9	3
Ensign staff	35	10	6
Jack staff	15	5	2½

The Admiralty promulgated a compulsory establishment of carronades on 19 November 1794, which laid down that 38-gun ships were to carry six 32-pounders on the quarterdeck with a further two on the forecastle. For the first time ships were to lose carriage guns to make room for them. *Diana* received 32-pounders on 23 February 1795 in place of her 18-pounders, but as she was only given six, not eight, she did not lose any of her 9-pounders. A further two 32-pounders were acquired later on and although circumstantial evidence suggests that no 9-pounders were given up in exchange it is not possible to confirm this. Although it has not been possible to establish the exact date when this addition was made, the most likely time would have been during the 1796 refit.

On 12 December 1799 the Admiralty ordered that all frigates, on refitting, were to have the carriage guns on their quarterdecks and forecastles replaced by carronades, with the exception of two, which were to be retained as chase guns. As a result of this *Diana*'s quarterdeck armament became twelve 32-pounder carronades and her forecastle armament became two 32-pounder carronades and two 9-pounder carriage guns. The most likely date for this to have taken place would have been during the 1801 refit.

This was probably the last change in the ship's armament, although a manuscript Navy List dated 1816 states that her forecastle carronades were 24-pounders. This is probably a clerical error. It was also out of date because *Diana* had been sold to the Dutch in 1815. However as she went into Ordinary in 1812 to await a 'very large repair' it is just possible that lighter weapons had been fitted prior to this, in order to reduce the strain on what by then was a very tired structure. It is very unlikely though, as the difference in weight between a 24- and 32-pounder carronade was only 2¾ hundredweight.

SERVICE HISTORY
First Commission (Captain Johnathon Faulknor – 19 April 1794 to 28 March 1799)

13 June 1794: 6½ weeks at the Nore working-up, and completing her crew.

27 July: sailed for the Downs. Joined there by sister ship *Artois*.

31 July: proceeded down Channel to join Sir John Warren's frigate squadron on the Irish station to help patrol south western approaches to the Channel, from southern Ireland to the French coast.

8 August: Plymouth harbour with *Diamond* and on 13th joined *Artois* at Falmouth.

15 August: joined Sir John Warren off Lizard, with rest of squadron.

23 August: fired first shot in anger – with her sisters and *Santa Margarita* drove French 36-gun ship *Volontaire* ashore on Penmarck rocks and her two consorts ashore further along the coast.

27 August: with the squadron recaptured two merchant vessels making for France.

September: with consorts from Sir Edward Pellew's squadron recaptured Swedish brig *Haesingland* and French cutter *La Quartidi*.

November–December: damaged by bad weather whilst on patrol.

23 January 1795: lost fore topmast and backstays and put into Scilly Isles for repairs.

End January: Plymouth Harbour 'making good defects' caused by bad weather on patrol in previous months.

February–June: almost continually at sea on Irish station.

25 June: Cork harbour for a month's repair work.

August: highlight of career. With sister ship *Seahorse* and frigate *Unicorn* captured Dutch East Indiaman *Cromhout*, another merchant ship *Hustelderk*, and their escort *Komeet*. £46,900 prize money from *Cromhout* alone.

7 December: after seven weeks' repairs at Spithead, sailed with convoy for Cork.

Late 1795 – May 1796: patrols in Irish waters. Was one of squadron which captured French cutter *L'Abeille* in May.

June: refit at Portsmouth

August: accompanied by *Seahorse* and *Cerberus* captured French privateer brig *L'Indemnite*, west of Finisterre.

Early November: shared in capture of French privateer *Le Franklin* – last event of note in 1796.

January – mid-May 1797: apart from spells in Cork, patrolled Western Approaches.

22–29 May: to Dungeness with convoy, captured 2 French fishing boats on way back.

June–July: at anchor in Spithead.

August: week at Weymouth as part of escort for the King.

September: with *Cerberus* captured privateer cutter *Le Neptun*, recaptured the merchant prize *Albion;* and *Kangeroo* captured privateers *Graff Bernstoff* and *San Norberto*, and on her own took the French privateer *L'Hibustion*

TABLE 6: BELAYING POINTS

Location (the letters used are those in drawings F5/10–12 with additions)

A – Taffarel
B – Mizen topsail sheet bitts
C – Mizen mast
D – Fore brace bitts
E – Quarterdeck breast rail
F – Main mast
G – After skid beam
H – Main jeer bitts
I – Main topsail sheet bitts
J – Forward skid beams
K – Forecastle breast rail
L – Belfry
M – Fore jeer bitts
N – Fore mast
O – Fore topsail sheet bitts
P – Breasthook pin rail
Q – Upper deck in the waist
R – See remarks column
S – Mizen channel
T – Main channel
U – Fore channel
V – Mizen pin rail
W – Main pin rail
X – Fore shrouds
Y – Gangway
Z – Forecastle

Side

L – Larboard side only
B – Both sides
S – Starboard side only

Type

B – Kevel block
C – Cleat
H – Knighthead
I – Iron pin
K – Keval cleat
R – Range cleat
S – Shroud cleat
T – Timberhead
W – Wooden pin
X – As convenient

No	Item	Locn	Side	Type	Remarks
Crossjack					
1	Truss pendant	C	L	C	
2	Nave line	B	B	—	
3	Braces	W	B	W	Starboard brace belays on larboard side and vice versa
4	Lifts	V	B	W	
Main course					
5	Truss pendants	F	B	C	
6	Nave line	F	—	C	
7	Jeers	H	B	—	
8	Outer tricing lines	W	B	W	
9	Inner tricing lines	W	B	W	
10	Braces	R	B	R	Quarterdeck
11	Lifts	R	B	B	Abreast mast
12	Leech lines	E	B	—	
13	Bunt lines	K	B	—	
14	Clue garnets	I	B	—	
15	Sheets	R	B	R	Quarterdeck
16	Tacks	Q	B	R	
17	Bowlines	Z	B	B	
18	Slablines	I	B	—	
Fore course					
19	Truss pendants	N	B	C	
20	Nave line	N	—	C	
21	Jeers	M	B	—	
22	Outer tricing lines	X	B	C	
23	Inner tricing lines	X	B	C	
24	Braces	D	B	B	
25	Lifts	R	B	B	Abreast mast
26	Leech lines	K	B	—	
27	Bunt lines	K	B	—	
28	Clue garnets	O	B	—	
29	Sheets	Q	B	R	
30	Tacks	R	B	C	Cathead
31	Bowlines	O	B	—	
32	Slablines	O	B	—	
Mizen topsail					
33	Lifts	V	B	W	
34	Halliard	R	S	B	Quarterdeck
35	Braces	A	B	C	
36	Clue lines	V	B	W	With 38 – bunt lines
37	Reef tackles	B	B	—	
38	Bunt lines	V	B	W	With 36 – clue lines
39	Bowlines	W	B	W	Starboard bowline belays on larboard side and vice versa
40	Sheets	B	B	—	
Main topsail					
41	Lifts	E	B	—	
42	Halliards	R	B	B	Quarterdeck
43	Braces	B	B	—	
44	Clue lines	E	B	—	
45	Reef tackles	E	B	—	
46	Bunt lines	E	B	—	
47	Bowlines	M	B	—	
48	Sheets	I	B	—	
Fore topsail					
49	Lifts	X	B	S	
50	Halliards	Z	B	B	
51	Braces	J	B	I	
52	Clue lines	X	B	S	
53	Reef tackles	M	B	—	
54	Bunt lines	X	B	S	
55	Bowlines	O	B	—	
56	Sheets	O	B	—	
Mizen topgallant sail					
57	Lifts	R	B	—	Shroud in mizen top
58	Halliards	B	L	—	
59	Braces	A	B	C	
60	Clue lines	R	B	S	Mizen shrouds
61	Bowlines	D	B	—	
62	Sheets	B	B	—	
Main topgallant sail					
63	Lifts	R	B	—	Shroud in main top
64	Halliards	D	L	—	
65	Braces	V	B	W	
66	Clue lines	E	B	—	
67	Bowlines	M	B	—	
68	Sheets	E	B	—	
Fore topgallant sail					
69	Lifts	R	B	—	Shroud in fore top
70	Halliards	M	B	—	
71	Braces	L	B	C	
72	Clue lines	X	B	S	
73	Bowlines	O	B	—	
74	Sheets	M	B	—	
Spritsail					
75	Braces	K	B	—	
76	Lifts	P	B	W	
77	Bunt lines	P	B	W	
78	Clue lines	P	B	W	
79	Sheets	Q	B	C	
Driver					
80	Throat halliard	R	S	C	Quarterdeck bulwark
81	Peak halliard	R	L	C	Quarterdeck bulwark
82	Vangs	A	B	C	
83	Boom sheet	R	—	C	Quarterdeck middle line
84	Guys	A	B	C	Taffarel fife rail
85	Topping lifts	C	B	C	
86	Peak brails	R	B	C	Quarterdeck bulwark
87	Middle brails	R	B	S	Mizen shrouds
88	Throat brails	C	B	C	
89	Foot brails	C	B	C	
90	Sheet	R	—	C	Driver boom

No	Item	Locn	Side	Type	Remarks
Mizen staysail					
91	Halliard	B	S	—	
92	Downhauler	D	S	—	
93	Sheets	V	B	W	
94	Brails	D	B	—	
Main staysail					
95	Halliard	W	S	W	
96	Downhauler	M	S	—	
97	Sheets	W	B	W	
Fore staysail					
98	Halliard	X	S	S	
99	Downhauler	P	S	W	
100	Sheets	Z	B	T	
Mizen topmast staysail					
101	Halliard	B	L		
102	Downhauler	D	L	—	
103	Sheets	V	B	W	
104	Tacks	W	B	W	
Main topmast staysail					
105	Halliard	W	L	W	
106	Downhauler	M	L	—	
107	Sheets	G	B	I	
108	Tacks	X	B	S	
109	Brails	M	B	—	
Fore topmast staysail					
110	Stay	M	L	—	
111	Halliard	X	L	S	
112	Downhauler	P	L	W	
113	Sheets	Z	B	T	
114	Outhauler	P	L	W	
Middle staysail					
115	Stay	D	S	—	
116	Halliard	W	S	W	
117	Downhauler	M	S	—	
118	Sheets	G	B	I	
119	Tacks	R	B	X	Fore top
120	Tricing line	R	—	X	Fore top
Jib					
121	Stay	M	S	—	
122	Halliard	X	S	S	
123	Downhauler	P	L	W	
124	Sheets	Z	B	T	
125	Inhauler	P	S	W	
126	Outhauler	P	S	W	
Mizen topgallant staysail					
127	Halliard	B	S	—	
128	Downhauler	R	—	—	Main top rail
129	Sheets	V	B	W	
130	Tacks	R	B	X	Main top
Main topgallant staysail					
131	Halliard	W	L	W	

No	Item	Locn	Side	Type	Remarks
132	Downhauler	R	—	—	Fore top rail
133	Sheets	G	B	I	
134	Tacks	R	B	X	Fore top
Main studding sail					
135	Topping lift	W	B	W	
136	Fore guy	Y	B	C	
137	After guy	S	B	X	
138	Martingale	T	B	X	
139	Outer halliard	W	B	W	
140	Inner halliard	W	B	W	
141	Fore tack	Q	B	C	
142	After tack	S	B	X	
143	Fore sheet	W	B	W	
144	After sheet	W	B	W	
Fore studding sail					
145	Topping lift	X	B	—	
146	Fore guy	Z	B	T	
147	After guy	T	B	X	
148	Martingale	U	B	X	
149	Outer halliard	X	B	—	
150	Inner halliard	X	B	—	
151	Fore tack	Z	B	H	
152	After tack	Q	B	C	
153	Fore sheet	X	B	—	
154	After sheet	X	B	—	
Main topmast studding sail					
155	Topping lift	W	B	W	
156	Brace	S	B	X	
157	Halliard	W	B	W	
158	Tack	S	B	X	
159	Fore sheet	W	B	W	
160	After sheet	W	B	W	
161	Downhauler	J	B	I	
Fore topmast studding sail					
162	Topping lift	X	B	—	
163	Brace	Y	B	C	
164	Halliard	X	B	—	
165	Tack	Y	B	C	
166	Fore sheet	X	B	—	
167	After sheet	X	B	—	
168	Downhauler	Z	B	T	
Main topgallant studding sail					
169	Halliard	R	B	—	Main top rail
170	Tack	S	B	X	
171	Fore sheet	R	B	—	Main topsail yard
172	After sheet	R	B	—	Shroud in main top
Fore topgallant studding sail					
173	Halliard	R	B	—	Fore top rail
174	Tack	T	B	X	
175	Fore sheet	R	B	—	Fore topsail yard
176	After sheet	R	B	—	Shroud in fore top

Note: The numbers used are those in drawings F5/10–12.

October: captured French privateer *Le Filibustier*.
December: captured *La Manche* in company with *Shannon*.
2 February – early April 1798: refit at Portsmouth.
21 April: arrived off Ushant.
21 May: ventured into harbour at Brest with *Triton* and counted no less than 14 ships of the line and 12 frigates trapped by the British blockade.

11 July – end September: at sea on Irish Station.
1–17 October: at Cork. A week later, back at sea she took her only prize for the year, *Dunkfelt*.
7 November: Milford Haven for repairs.
21 November: arrived back at Cork for 6 weeks.
4 January – 8 February 1799: first patrol of the year on Irish station.

6 March: reached Scilly Isles with convoy from Cork.

28 March: moored off Southsea Castle where Captain Fraser relieved Captain Faulknor.

Second Commission (Captain Alexander Fraser – 29 March 1799 to 11 June 1800; Lieutenant Nott – 12 June 1800 to 12 July 1800; Captain John Poo Beresford – 13 July 1800 to 21 October 1801)

30 March: Portsmouth Dockyard for 2½ month refit, followed by working-up in Spithead.

6 September: sailed as part of an escort for a convoy bound for the West Indies where she was to spent two years on local convoys and patrolling amongst the islands, mainly intercepting and examining small craft engaged in fishing or inter-island trade.

11 November: Left Carlisle Bay with those ships which were not staying at Barbadoes. Worked her way to the Leeward Islands dropping off ships on the way.

26 November: Left St Kitts and was almost continually at sea for the rest of the year.

January – May 1800: constant patrolling of the West Indies – mostly uneventful.

12 May: recaptured an American schooner; 16 May recaptured an American sloop and on 17 May captured the privateer *La Medie* which had taken the former vessels.

12 June: Lieutenant Nott acting captain, relieving Captain Fraser who, like many of the crew, had yellow fever and had been invalided home.

25 June: recaptured American brig *William of Baltimore* and four days later the privateer *L'Industrie*.

13 July: John Poo Beresford replaced Lt Nott. Patrols continued in same pattern into early 1801.

28 February 1801: took French privateer *Le Triumphant*.

5 March: took unarmed schooner.

8 March: with *Amphitrite* sent boats inshore to cut out two launches and a ship from under the guns of St Jago and on 11 March captured Spanish brig *Actaeon*.

28 March: anchored off Danish island St Thomas's and fired on the Grand Battery, which struck its colours. Rear Admiral Duckworth's squadron sent in flag of truce. St Thomas's, St Johns and several smaller islands surrendered 29 March.

May onwards: resumed patrolling.

1 August: sailed for Britain with convoy of 190 ships

25 September: anchored in Spithead having delivered convoy to the Downs.

2 October: Portsmouth for refit and re-coppering, new main and mizen mast.

Third Commission (Captain Thomas James Maling – 22 October 1801 to 28 October 1807)

12 October: declaration of end of hostilities with France.

15 December: sailed for Mediterranean.

27 January 1802: sailed from Malta with *Northumberland* and *Bonne Citoyenne*.

9 February – 19 April: at anchor in Corfu Roads.

29 April: peace proclaimed in London.

21 April: two months at Malta.

5 July: sailed for Naples, then back to Malta before sailing eastwards.

2 September: reached Smyrna Bay. Spent two months cruising amongst Greek islands, returning to Smyrna at end of October.

10 November: Constantinople and then up the Bosphorus.

28 November– 7 January 1803: Beukdryh (Buyükdere)

16 January: Lord Elgin's baggage and horses embarked at Constantinople. He embarked on 17th and *Diana* sailed for home.

18 May: hostilities recommenced with France.

3 June: arrived at Spithead towing the French brig *L'Euphrosyne*, captured two days previously on her way up the Channel.

4 July: Two-week cruise in the Channel; intercepted two ships on passage from America to Germany.

4 August: escorted homecoming convoy of 22 ships from Lisbon.

26 September: reached the Downs, having captured Spanish ship and French brig *Le Jean Marie*. Escorted another convoy up the Channel to the Downs.

4 December: sailed from St Helens with convoy to Lisbon and the Mediterranean.

21 January 1804: Reached Gibraltar and spent a month in vicinity intercepting coastal shipping.

24 February: left Gibraltar with homeward bound convoy, losing one ship, which had sprung a leak, on the way.

8 April – 9 June: repairs and re-coppering at Portsmouth.

21 June: sailed for Cork to collect convoy for the West Indies.

24 July: left Madeira with enlarged convoy and 3 more escorts: *Beaulieu, Bacchante* and *Kingfisher*.

6 September: arrived Port Royal, Jamaica.

13 September: first cruise of many in West Indies, eastwards along coast of St Domingo, south to Dutch islands off South America. During this time captured Spanish schooner and brig and with *Echo* accepted the surrender of the island of Aruba.

20 November: returned to Port Royal with captured sloop and four other prizes.

6 December: sailed with *Suffisante*. The Spanish *Diligentia* surrendered on the 21st after being chased by *Diana* and *La Pique*.

January – March 1805: Island of Aruba as base. Took numerous prizes and recaptured 3 American vessels.

April: fitting out at Port Royal.

28 April – 3 September: cruised westwards.

30 September – 21 October: after a month in harbour at Port Royal, sailed to north coast of Jamaica. Sent two prizes home to Falmouth.

2 November: to sea, heading for Britain with 24-ship convoy assisted by 18-gun brig sloop *Port Mahon*. Anchored in Port Antonio and joined by a further 17 ships and two more escorts *Bacchante* and *Wolf*.

23 February – 16 April 1806: refit at Portsmouth.

12 May: sailed from St Helen's with convoy for Gibraltar, collecting more ships, including *Richmond*, from Falmouth on the way, making a total of 60. On 24 May *Richmond* left with 9 ships for Oporto and on 29 May Lisbon portion of convoy departed.

8 June: squall carried away mizzen topmast and main topgallant yard two days into return passage to Spithead.

1 August: sailed from Cork to cruise in Atlantic with *Dryad* and *Princess Charlotte*.

26 September: severe storm in Atlantic snapped bowsprit which brought down fore mast, main and mizen topmasts. 9 killed and 25 injured in clearing wreckage. Turned back under jury rig, whilst repairs were made.

10 October: repairs at Portsmouth for 2½ months.

5 January 1807: convoy to Cork followed by several months in Channel approaches.

18 February: captured *Charlotte*.

15 March: quarter watch allowed ashore at Bear Island, but 15 deserted.

April: captured Guernsey smugglers *Dart* and *Eliza*.

30 April – 12 May: spell as Admiral Lord Gardner's flagship,; passage to Portsmouth.

27 May: sailed with two supernumeries for Jamaica. Uneventful, except for grounding off Porto Rico.

7 July: sailed for Vera Cruz and by 27th had six prizes in company and one in tow.

2 August: anchored off Vera Cruz; sent boat ashore with flag of truce. Embarked 1273 boxes and 14 bags of dollars.

24 August – 19 October: passage home in company with *John* and *Thames*, uneventful.

Fourth Commission (Captain Charles Grant – 29 October 1807 to 11 April 1811)

30 October – 31 December: repairs and re-coppering at Portsmouth

January – April 1808: cruised independently off Biscay coast. 4 February took schooner off Cordovan Light. 6 February reconnoitred Basque Roads and captured two chasse-marées. End February captured galliot *Naphousan*.

March: successful month, took or destroyed 18 vessels.

27 April: Plymouth for repairs and stores.

18 May: departed for vicinity of Finnistere. Uneventful patrolling until December, the only break being in July when she accompanied a convoy to Oporto.

17–31 January 1809: docked at Plymouth and then in Plymouth Sound.

12 March: sailed for South America with Rear Admiral the Honourable Michael de Courcy who was to relieve Sir Sidney Smith as Flag Officer, Brazil.

15 March: recaptured brig *Hayti*.

1 May: reached Rio de Janeiro. Sir Sidney embarked. Loaded bullion for three weeks.

21 June: Left Rio, accompanied by *Cheerly* and *Nancy*. Recaptured Spanish *Santa Francisco de Paulo*.

9 August: Anchored at Spithead. Admiral's flag struck, and on 11th the specie was discharged.

27 August: Sailed with *Nereus* and *Brilliant* to patrol coast between Boulogne and Dieppe.

5 October: Captain Grant temporarily superseded by Captain Cramer, probably due to illness. Channel patrol.

22 October: arrived at Flushing with 40 women for the army.

23 November: moored at Barcelen (Borsselen) upstream from Flushing for three weeks.

16 February 1810: sailed for Bay of the Seine. Continuous blockade for 12 months, for first 7 months broken only by monthly visits to Spithead.

12 November: *Diana* and *Niobe* intercepted two French frigates *L'Amazone* and *L'Elize* and drove them into La Hogue Roads. After bombardment by *Diana*, *Niobe*, *Donegal* and *Revenge*, *L'Elize* was hard aground and *L'Amazone* a complete wreck. *Diana* and *Niobe* remained in the vicinity for five weeks.

23–24 December: *Diana's* boats went in at night and set fire to *L'Elize*.

19 February – 6 April 1811: Plymouth for re-coppering and repairs.

Fifth commission (Captain William Ferris – 12 April 1811 to 2 May 1812)

20 May: arrived Biscay coast on last commission in Royal Navy. Two months as part of force blockading Rochefort.

21 July: put to sea. Five weeks beating back and forth in vicinity of Cordovan Light blockading upstream port of Bordeaux.

24 August: incident at mouth of Gironde, whilst in company with *Semiramis*, which resulted in retaking the former British brig *Teazer* and destroying the French brig *Le Pluvier*. Boats took many prizes. Remained on patrol off Cordovan Light.

15 September: Plymouth, repairs.

11 November: sailed for French blockade. Apart from brief return to Portsmouth remained on patrol off Ushant until end of March 1812.

2 May 1912 – 3 March 1813: end of career with Royal Navy. In Ordinary at Plymouth.

19 March: On slip at Blackburn for 'very large repair'.

30 May 1814: Britain and France signed peace treaty.

29 November: Left dock after coppering and fitted for sea.

7 March 1815: sold to Dutch Government for £36,796.

19 May: sailed from Portsmouth for the last time. Joined Dutch Navy in the Mediterranean.

27 August 1816: one of six frigates of Dutch squadron that combined with British fleet to take part in bombardment of Algiers.

Late 1816: returned to Netherlands.

1819 and 1826: back in Mediterranean.

10 November 1834: sailed to Dutch East Indies with Governor General Elect of East Indies.

December 1835: New Guinea.

April 1836: Key Islands.

5 August: Batavia to Texel, making record time for passage.

16 January 1839: destroyed by accidental fire in drydock at Willemsoord.

SOURCES

At the National Maritime Museum
    ADM/A series – Navy Board, In letters and orders
    ADM/B series – Admiralty, In letters
    ADM/L series – Lieutenants' logs
    LOG/N/D/12 – Log, author unknown
    DOU/100 – Log, Midshipman Douglas
    ADM/168 series – Ships' contracts (ADM/168/149 – *Artois* class)
    AND 35 – Notebook 1793; illustrations and explanations related to ship-building
    SPB series – Miscellaneous documents concerning shipbuilding
              Admiralty Collection draughts

At the Public Record Office
    ADM/8 series – List books
    ADM/36 series – Ships' musters
    ADM/51 series – Captains' logs
    ADM/52 series – Masters' logs
    ADM/95 series – Controller's Office miscellanea (Navy Board warrants)
    ADM/106 series – Navy Board In letters (Standing orders to Dockyards and Surveyor's Office minutes)
    ADM/112 series – Contract ledgers
    ADM/180 series – Progress books

The Photographs

All the photographs are reproduced by courtesy of the National Maritime Museum, which has three models of *Diana*. Two of them, numbers 1794–2 and 1794–2a, are virtually identical and were undoubtedly built by the same hand. The third one, number 1794–3, differs in detail and shows signs of a different modelmaker. All these models are preliminary ones; they do not represent the ship as built.

2. Model number 1794–2. The starboard side of the ship on her launching cradle. One of the principal differences between this model and 1794–2a is that this one has no riders.

3. The stern of 1794–2 demonstrating the run of the hull planking. The decoration on the stern of this model is identical to that of 1794–2a but differs from the ship as built.

4. This overhead view of 1794–2a gives a good impression of the lines of the hull and the layout of the decks. The model lacks the chesstrees that can be seen on 1794–2.

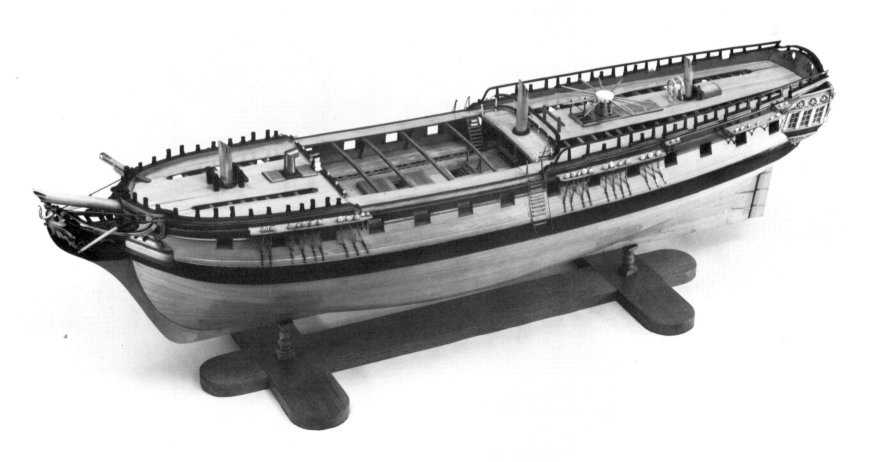

5. 1794–2a from the larboard quarter. This model is the only one to have rudder chains, gangway stanchions and entering ropes.

6. A broadside view of 1794–3. This model has far more detail than the other two. Amongst the more obvious items are gun port lids, oar ports, various eyebolts below the channels, fenders, bill board, leaded gripe and scuppers. The decoration on the quarter galleries and the two dogs on the trailboard are very similar to those on the ship as built.

Apart from two items this model is the nearest one to the actual ship as built. The first difference is in the curve of the gripe, which is much sharper than it is on the other models. The latter agree with the draughts. Secondly, it has crutches for temporary skid beams instead of having permanent ones, a feature long obsolete by the time that *Diana* was built. The most likely explanation for this is that the original design for the class followed close behind that of the *Minerva*s of the early 1780s and that when the war ended in 1782 it was not pursued further. This model probably dates from then.

When the French Revolutionary War commenced in 1793 the design was resurrected and two further, more austere, models were made. One of them, 1794–2a, was made for the Surveyor, Sir John Henslow. It remained in the possession of the Henslow family until 1957, when Mrs E Henslow presented it to the museum.

7, 8. Two pictures of a model of *Minerva*, the ship from which *Diana* and her sisters were developed. This model, quite rightly, has crutches for portable skid beams. One of the more noticeable, although minor, differences between the two classes is the position of the quarterdeck breastwork. In *Minerva* it is ahead of the mainmast; in *Diana* it is abaft it.

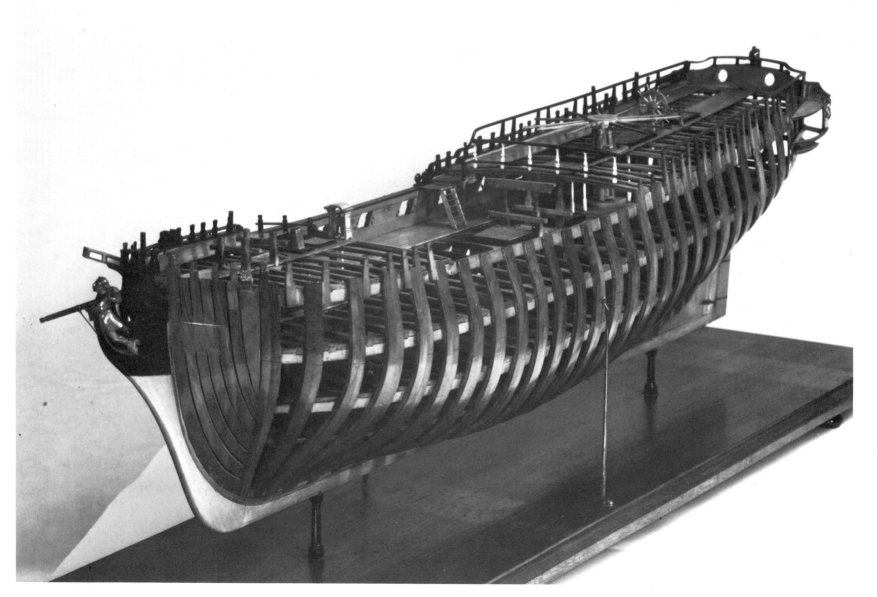

9, 10. The model in these two photographs is of a 32-gun frigate of 1780. However apart from the hawse pieces having boxing on them the construction is virtually the same as *Diana*'s. Note that there are no filling frames; they have been omitted for the sake of clarity.

11, 12. The model depicted here is usually described as a 36-gun frigate c1805 but the hull has characteristics of detail which place it between 1796 and 1800. The rigging, which is believed to be original, is almost identical to that of *Diana*.

The Drawings

SOURCES

The drawings in this section are the tip of an iceberg built up as a result of more than thirty-five years' research. They are, of course, all reconstructions, most of them of drawings which never existed when the ship was built. Those that appear in the following pages are part of what is believed to be the largest and most accurate collection of plans of the classic frigate to ever exist.

The study has been largely based on the Admiralty Collection in the Draught Room of the National Maritime Museum at Greenwich. There are around eight thousand draughts in this collection, of which roughly one-quarter relate to frigates. Thirty-eight of these are of the *Artois* class ships and according to the catalogue ten of them represent *Diana*. However, this is not so. Draught number 1883, the sheer draught, is the original Navy Board copy for building the class and has several projected modifications overdrawn on it – one of them for a 36-gun version. The inside and outside planking expansions, draughts numbers 1884 and 1884A, remain mysteries. They are dated 'Deptford Yard 14 May 08' and as far as can be ascertained no ship of the class was ever in the state depicted. Circumstantial evidence in other fields points to them being academic exercises only.

Many other channels have been explored and re-explored to obtain accurate and authentic information. Some of the major ones are listed at the end of the Introduction under the heading 'Sources'. To list them all would require a further volume.

The scales are based on the standard ¼ inch = 1 foot (1/48th) utilized in Admiralty draughts of the period, with details in multiples thereof – 1/96 being ⅛ inch = 1 foot, 1/192 being ¹⁄₁₆ inch = 1 foot, and so on.

A Lines and arrangement

A1   LINES

A1/1   Sheer draught (1/192 scale, except body plan 1/96)

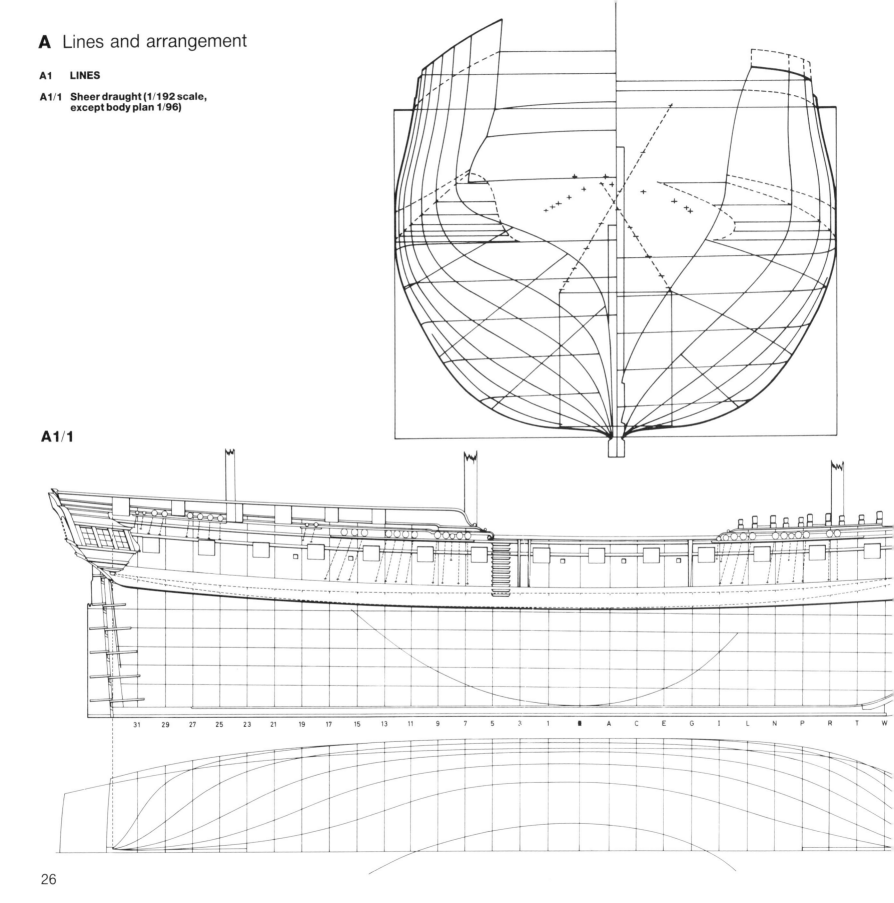

A1/1

31 29 27 25 23 21 19 17 15 13 11 9 7 5 3 1 ■ A C E G I L N P R T W

A1/2 Perspective (no scale)
1. Toptimber line
2. Sheer line
3. Heights of breadth
4. Waterlines
5. Rabbet
6. Joint line

A1/2

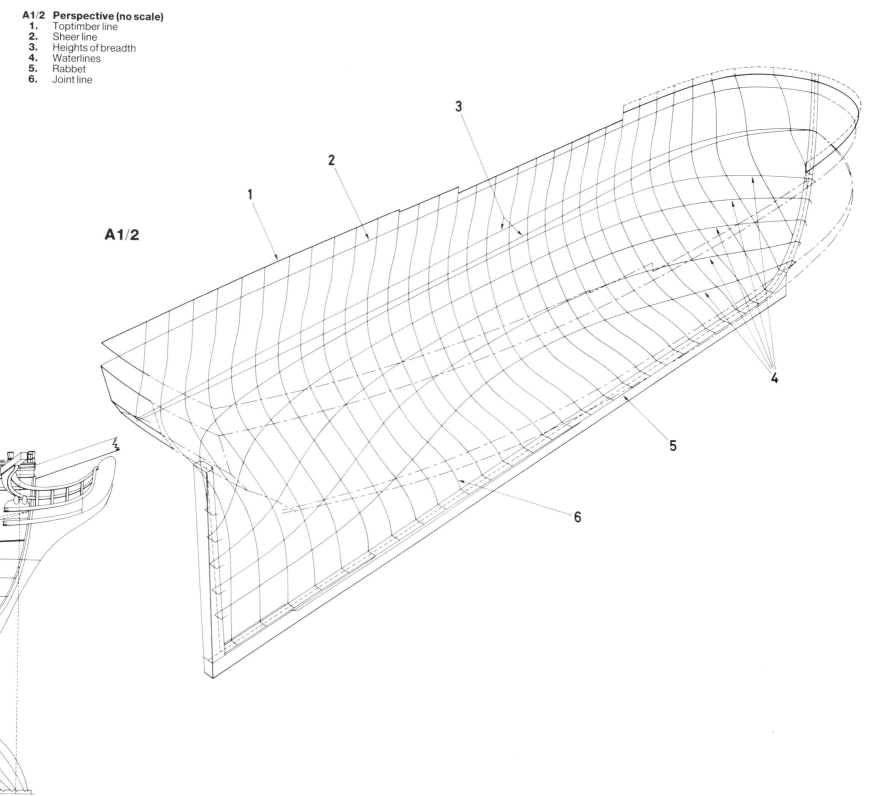

A Lines and arrangement

A1/3

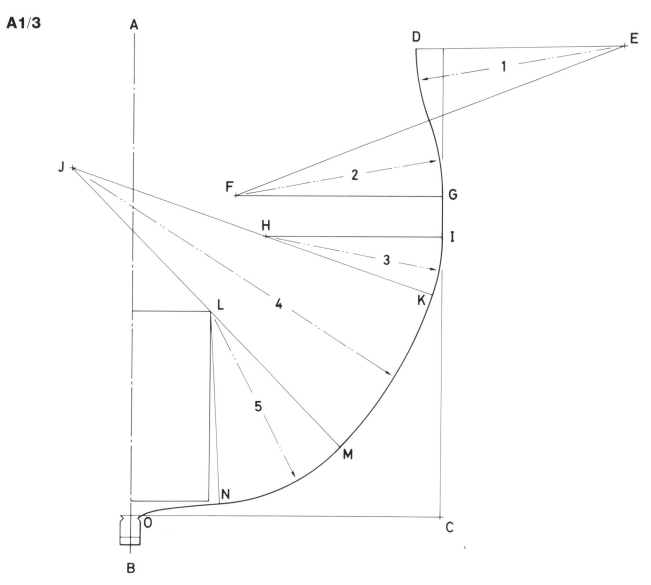

A1/3 **Draughting the midship section (no scale)**

1.	Radius of the toptimber sweep
2.	Radius of the upper breadth sweep
3.	Radius of the lower breadth sweep
4.	Radius of the reconciling sweep
5.	Radius of the floor sweep
AB	Middle line
OC	Rabbet line
DG	Toptimber sweep
E,F	Centres of the toptimber sweeps
GI	Maximum breadth
IK	Lower breadth sweep
H	Centre of the lower breadth sweep
KM	Reconciling sweep
J	Centre of the reconciling sweep
MN	Floor sweep
L	Centre of the floor sweep and the rising line of centres of the floor sweep
NO	Rise of floor

A2   GENERAL ARRANGEMENT

A2/1 Perspective (no scale)
  1. Quarterdeck
  2. Gangway
  3. Forecastle
  4. Stern post
  5. Keel
  6. Wale
  7. Upper deck

A2/1

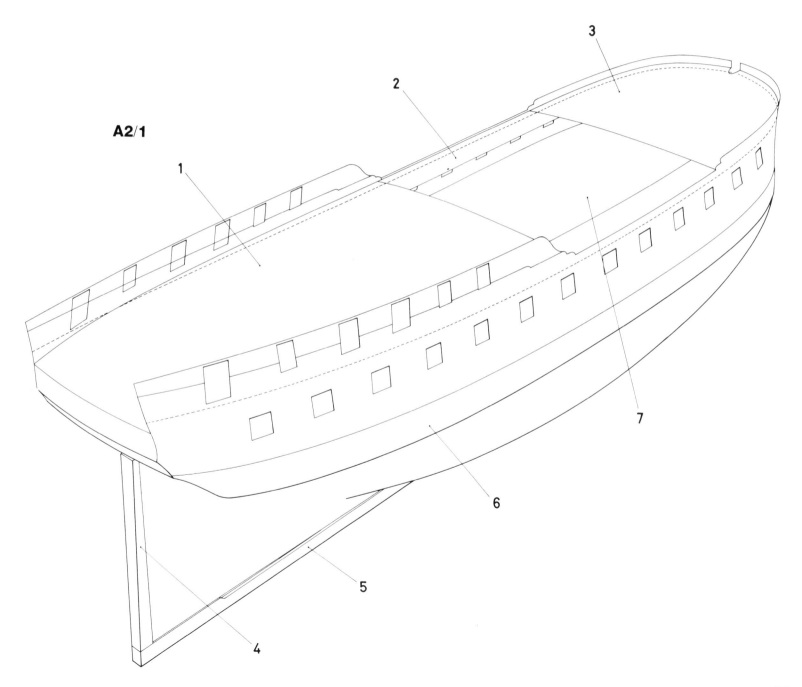

A Lines and arrangement

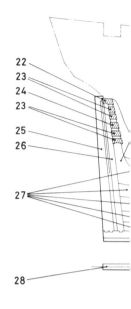

A2/2 Profile (1/192 scale)

1.	Quarterdeck	18.	Wardroom
2.	Great cabin	19.	Bread room
3.	Upper deck	20.	Lower deck
4.	Companion	21.	After magazine
5.	Wheel	22.	After platform
6.	Coach (larboard), bedplace (starboard)	23.	Fish room
		24.	Spirit room
7.	Capstan	25.	After hold
8.	Main jeer bitts	26.	Shot lockers
9.	Barricade	27.	Pump shaft
10.	Main topsail sheet bitts	28.	Well
11.	Main hatchway	29.	Orlop
12.	Fore hatchway	30.	Main hold
13.	Riding bitts	31.	Cable tier
14.	Belfry	32.	Fore hold
15.	Galley stove	33.	Forward magazine
16.	Fore jeer bitts	34.	Fore platform
17.	Fore topsail sheet bitts	35.	Filling room
		36.	Light room

A2/2

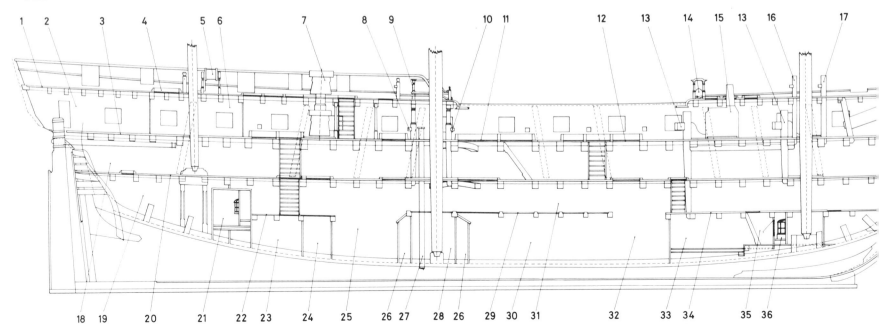

B Hull structure

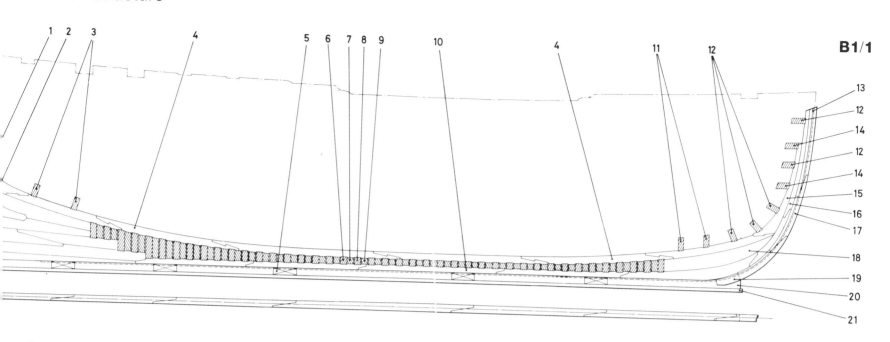

B1/1

B1/2

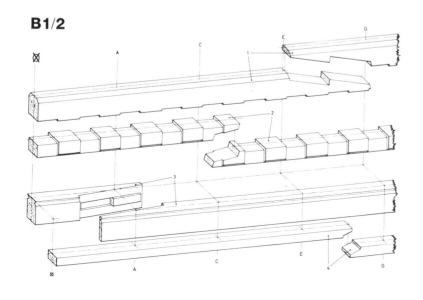

B1/3

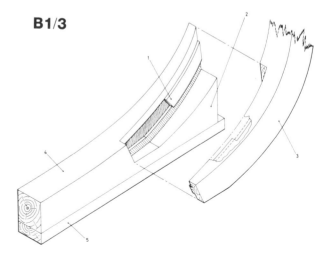

B Hull structure

B1/4

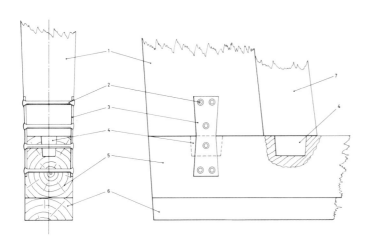

B1/5

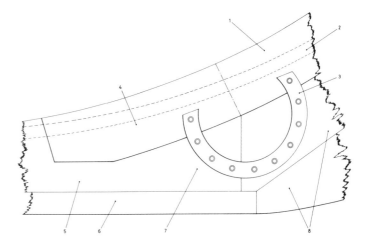

B2/1

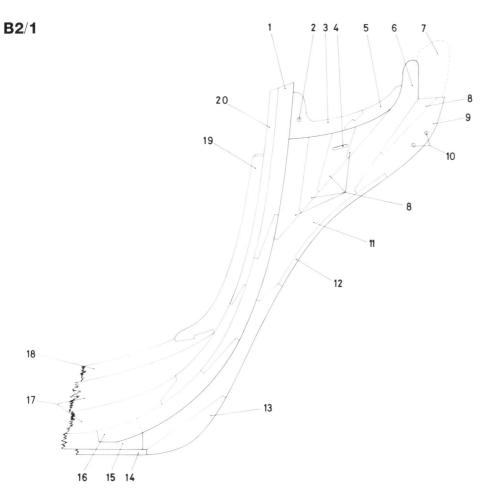

B1/4 Fastening the stern post to the keel (1/16 scale)
1. Stern post
2. Bolts
3. Copper horseshoe plate
4. Tenon
5. Keel
6. False keel
7. Inner post

B1/5 Horseshoe plate (1/16 scale)
1. Stem
2. Rabbet
3. Horseshoe plate
4. Boxing
5. Keel
6. False keel
7. Forefoot
8. Gripe

B2 BOW

B2/1 Stem and knee of the head (1/96 scale)
1. Stem
2. Hole for the mainstay collar
3. Gammoning knee or standard
4. Gammoning slot
5. Ekeing
6. Lacing
7. Block
8. Chocks
9. Bobstay piece
10. Bobstay holes
11. Main piece
12. Face piece
13. Gripe
14. False keel
15. Forefoot
16. Boxing
17. Deadwood
18. Keelson
19. Stemson
20. Apron

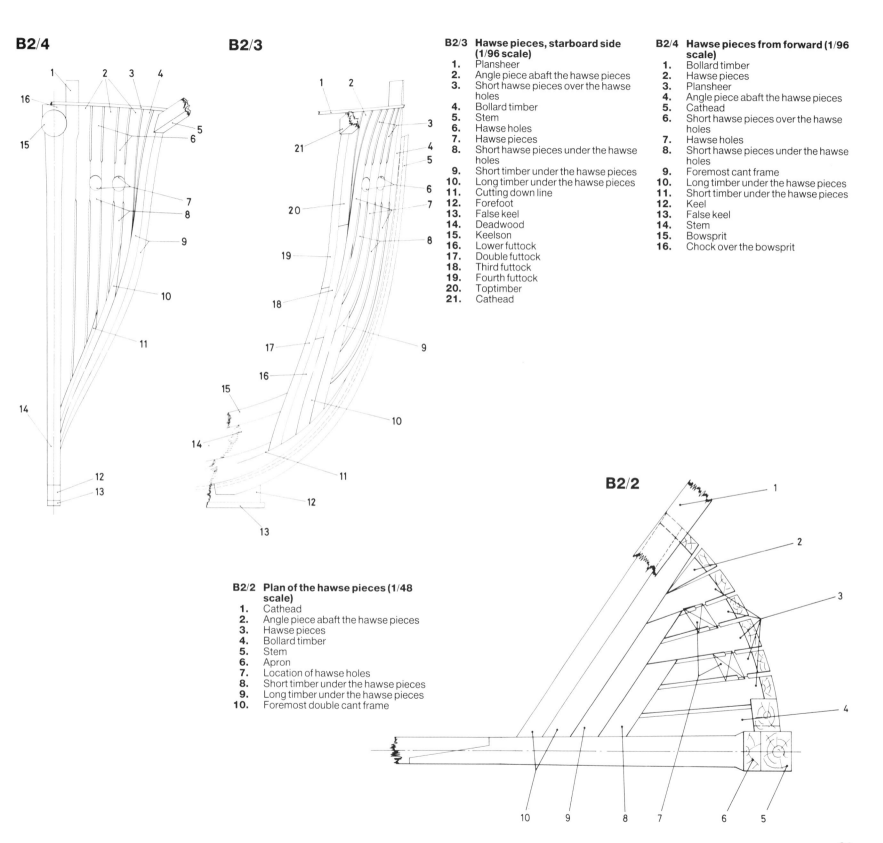

B2/4

B2/3

B2/2

B Hull structure

B3/1

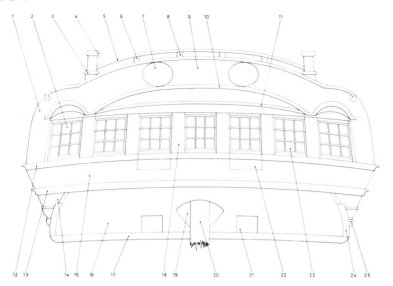

B3 STERN AND STERN FRAME

B3/1 Stern from aft (1/96 scale)
1. Quarter piece
2. Quarter gallery false light
3. Plansheer
4. Rough tree rail
5. Taffarel fife rail
6. Middle counter timber
7. Quarterdeck chase port
8. Midship counter timber
9. Taffarel
10. Cove
11. Necking
12. Upper counter rail
13. Lower counter rail
14. Lower finishing
15. Upper counter
16. Lower counter
17. Wing transom
18. Munnion
19. Helm port
20. Rudder
21. Lower deck port
22. Upper deck chase port lid
23. Great cabin sash light
24. Wale
25. Drop

B3/2 Stern, starboard side (1/96 scale)
1. Taffarel fife rail
2. Rough tree rail
3. Plansheer
4. Fretwork to the upper finishing
5. Quarterdeck carronade port
6. Upper finishing
7. Quarter gallery sash light
8. Upper stool rail
9. Console bracket (canting livre)
10. Quarterdeck gun port
11. Quarterdeck berthing
12. Taffarel
13. Quarter piece
14. Upper counter rail
15. Upper counter
16. Lower counter rail
17. Quarter gallery false lights
18. Rim rail
19. Rudder
20. Stern post
21. Tuck rail
22. Drop
23. Lower finishing
24. Lower stool rail
25. Quarter gallery berthing
26. Wale
27. Upper deck gun ports

B3/2

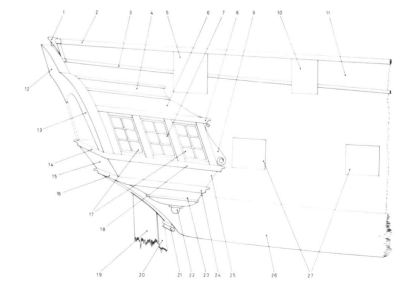

B3/3 Plan of the stern (1/96 scale)

1. Quarter piece
2. Fretwork to the upper finishing
3. Upper finishing
4. Upper stool rail
5. False lights
6. Sash light
7. Munnion
8. Rim rail
9. Quarterdeck carronade port
10. Upper deck gun port
11. Rough tree rail
12. Quarterdeck gun port
13. Taffarel
14. Taffarel fife rail
15. Quarterdeck chase port
16. Quarterdeck transom
17. Flat of quarterdeck
18. Companion

B3/3

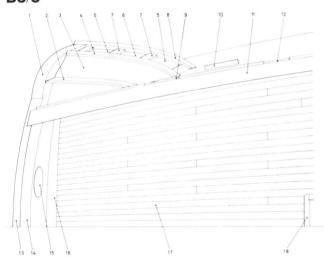

B3/4

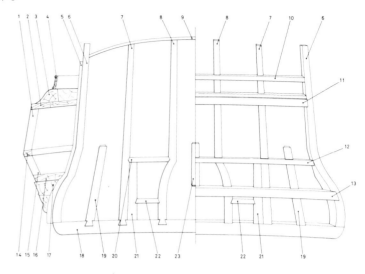

B3/4 Framing of the stern (left — from aft; right — from forward, omitting the quarter gallery; 1/96 scale)

1. Munnion
2. Upper stool
3. Upper finishing
4. Fretwork to the upper finishing
5. Outer planking of hull
6. Side counter timber
7. Middle counter timber
8. Midship counter timber
9. Taffarel fife rail
10. Transom on the quarterdeck
11. Quarterdeck transom
12. Seat transom
13. Upper deck transom
14. Rim
15. Stanchion for the berthing
16. Lower stool
17. Lower finishing
18. Wing transom
19. Short counter timber
20. Lower sill of upper deck chase port
21. Filling piece
22. Upper sill of lower deck port
23. Short counter timber

B Hull structure

B3/5

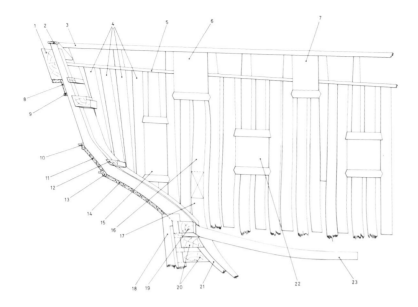

B3/5 Framing of the stern (middle line section, 1/96 scale)

1. Taffarel
2. Taffarel fife rail
3. Rough tree rail
4. Timbers on the side counter timber
5. Plansheer
6. Quarterdeck carronade port
7. Quarterdeck gun port
8. Cove
9. Necking
10. Upper counter rail
11. Upper counter (second counter)
12. Seat transom
13. Lower counter rail
14. Lower counter
15. Gallery doorway
16. Scarphed extension to forward fashion piece
17. Forward fashion piece
18. Stern post
19. Wing transom
20. Filling transom
21. After fashion piece
22. Upper deck gun port
23. Wing transom knee

B3/6 Framing of the stern, (plan, 1/96 scale)

1. Midship counter timber
2. Middle counter timber
3. Transom on the quarterdeck
4. Short counter timber
5. Seat transom
6. Side counter timber
7. Upper deck transom
8. Wing transom
9. Wing transom knee
10. Lower deck clamp
11. Quarterdeck transom
12. Short counter timber
13. Helm port
14. Chock to upper deck transom
15. After fashion piece
16. Forward fashion piece
17. Deadwood

B3/6

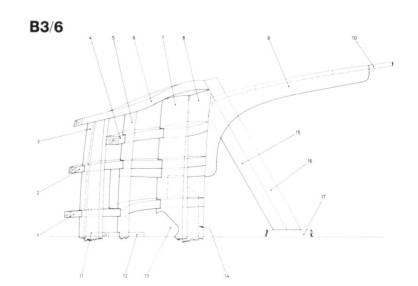

B3/7 Stern frame from aft (1/96 scale)
1. Forward fashion piece
2. Wing transom
3. Stern post
4. Filling transom
5. After fashion piece
6. Deck transom
7. Filling transoms
8. Chocks under the transoms
9. Inner post
10. Deadwood
11. Keel

B3/8 Stern frame from starboard (1/96 scale)
1. Forward fashion piece
2. After fashion piece
3. Deadwood
4. Wing transom
5. Filling transoms
6. Deck transom
7. Filling transoms
8. Chocks under the transoms
9. Rabbet
10. Stern post
11. Inner post
12. False keel

B3/9 Section of the upper counter rail (1/4 scale)

B3/10 Section of the lower counter rail (1/4 scale)

B3/11 Section of the tuck rail (1/4 scale)

B3/7

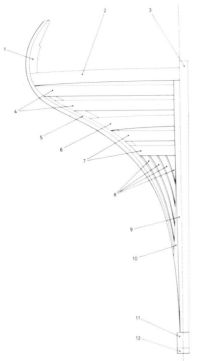

B3/8

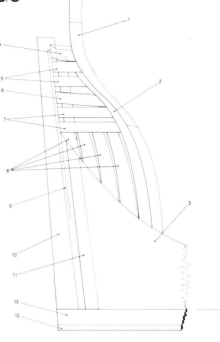

B3/9

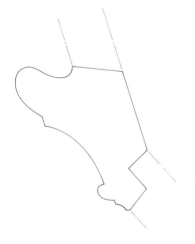

B3/10

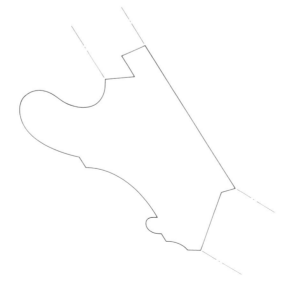

B3/11

B Hull structure

B4 FRAMES

B4/1 Profile and half breadth (1/192 scale)

The main drawings show the ship with three quarterdeck carronade ports as fitted 1796, but with hawse pieces as originally designed (for hawse pieces as built see B2/2,3,4). The partial view shows the ship as originally built with two quarterdeck carronade ports.

1. Carronade port
2. 9-pounder gun port
3. 18-pounder gun port
4. Oar port
5. Inserted timberheads
6. Side counter timber
7. Quarter gallery door
8. Wing transom
9. Deck transom
10. Filling transom
11. Stern post
12. After fashion piece
14. After deadwood
15. Hawse holes
16. Hawse pieces as originally designed
17. Bollard timbers (knightheads)
18. Stem
19. Forward deadwood
20. Keel
21. False keel
22. Cathead
23. Floor
24. Lower futtock
25. Second futtock
26. Third futtock
27. Fourth futtock
28. Toptimber
29. After cant frames
30. Forward cant frames
31. Counter timbers

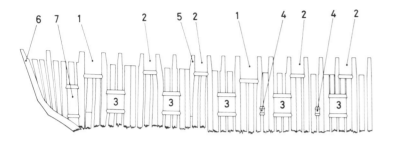

B4/1

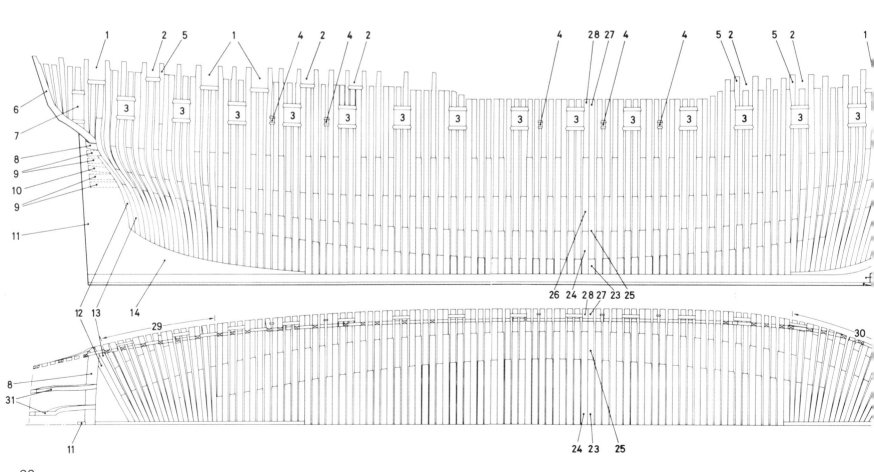

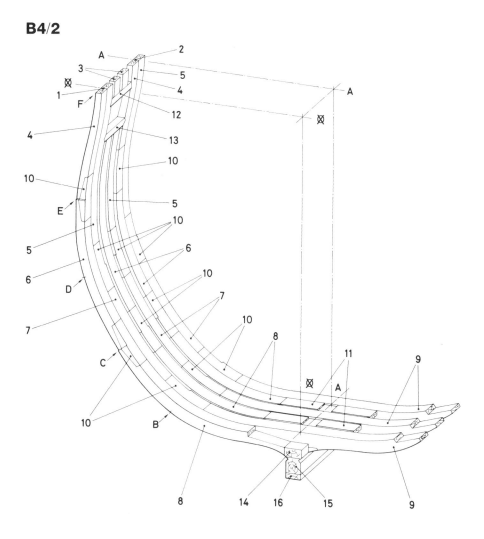

B4/2

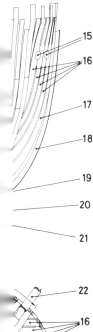

B Hull structure

B4/3

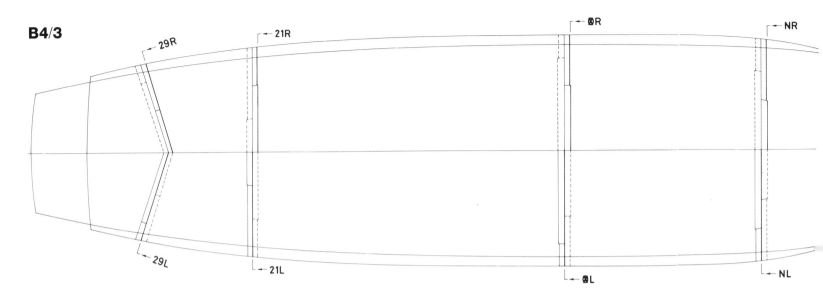

B4/3 Location plan of the frame bends in B4/4 to B4/7 (1/192 scale)

B4/4 Components of the midship bend from forward (left – abaft the joint line; right – forward of the joint line; 1/96 scale)

1. Toptimber
2. Chock
3. Third futtock
4. Lower futtock
5. Fourth futtock
6. Second futtock
7. Floor
8. Keelson
9. Floor chock
10. Rising wood
11. Keel
12. False keel
13. Cross chock

B4/4

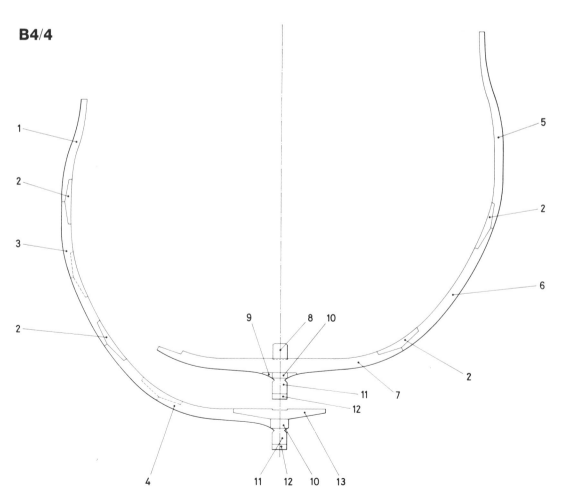

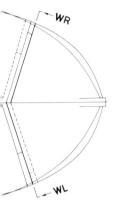

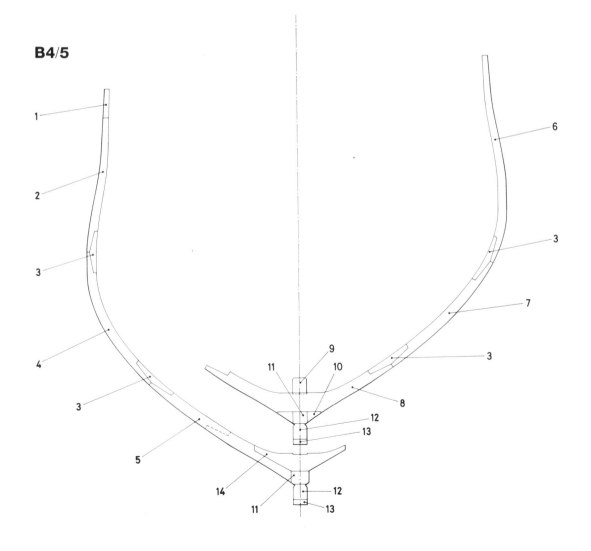

B4/5 Components of bend N from forward (left – abaft the joint line; right – forward of the joint line; 1/96 scale)

1. Extension to toptimber forming timberhead
2. Toptimber
3. Chock
4. Third futtock
5. First futtock
6. Fourth futtock
7. Second futtock
8. Floor
9. Keelson
10. Floor chock
11. Rising wood
12. Keel
13. False keel
14. Cross chock

B4/5

B Hull structure

B4/6

B4/7

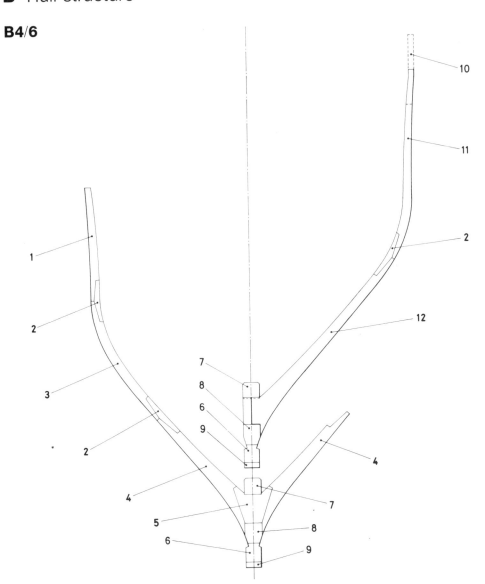

B4/6 Components of cant frame bend W from forward (left – abaft the joint line; right – forward of the joint line; 1/96 scale)

1. Toptimber
2. Chock
3. Third futtock
4. First futtock
5. Cross chock
6. Keel
7. Keelson
8. Deadwood
9. False keel
10. Timberhead
11. Fourth futtock
12. Second futtock

B4/8

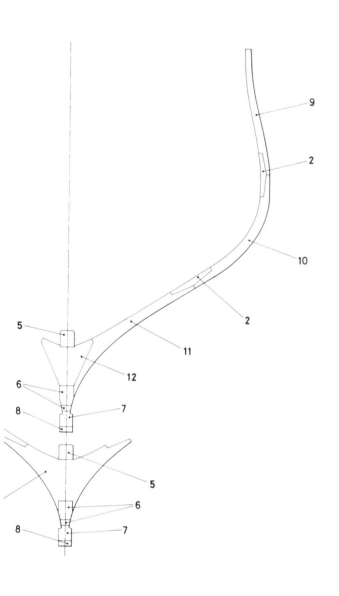

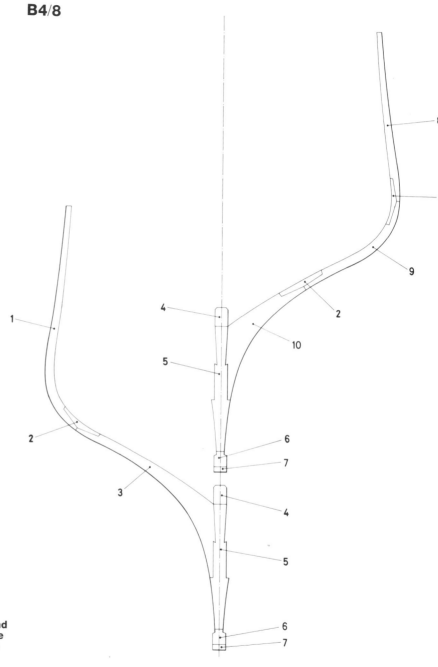

B4/7 **Components of bend 21 from forward (left – abaft the joint line; right – forward of the joint line; 1/96 scale)**

1. Fourth futtock
2. Chock
3. Second futtock
4. Floor
5. Keelson
6. Deadwood
7. Keel
8. False keel
9. Toptimber
10. Third futtock
11. Lower futtock
12. Cross chock

B4/8 **Components of cant frame bend 29 from forward (left – abaft the joint line; right – forward of the joint line; 1/96 scale)**

1. Fourth futtock
2. Chock
3. Second futtock
4. Keelson
5. After deadwood
6. Keel
7. False keel
8. Toptimber
9. Third futtock
10. Lower futtock

C Internal hull

C1 ARRANGEMENTS

C1/1 Position of decks, in perspective (no scale)

1. Quarterdeck
2. Gangway
3. Forecastle
4. After platform
5. Lower deck
6. Orlop
7. Upper deck
8. Fore platform

C1/1

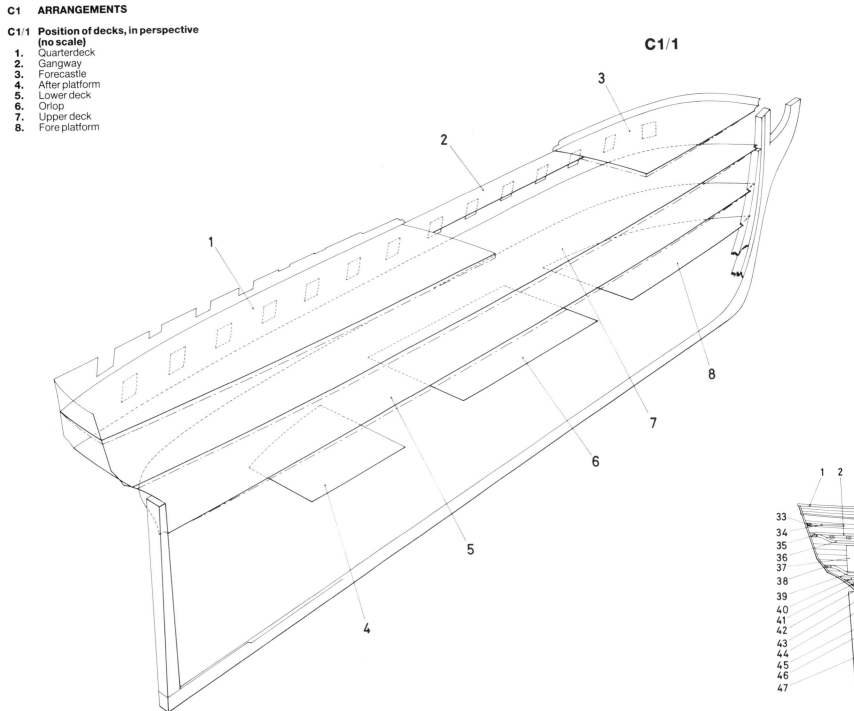

C1/2 Hull at side (1/192 scale)

1. Rough tree rail
2. Quarterdeck waterway
3. 32-pounder carronade port
4. 18-pounder gun port
5. 9-pounder gun port
6. Quarterdeck berthing
7. Quarterdeck plansheer
8. Quarterdeck clamp
9. Iron hanging tree
10. Top rider
11. Iron cast knee
12. Quarterdeck spirketting
13. Wooden dagger knee
14. Oar port
15. Wooden hanging knee
16. Iron dagger knee
17. Quarterdeck breast beam
18. Gunwale
19. Skid beam
20. String

21. Forecastle breast beam
22. Forecastle plansheer
23. Forecastle spirketting
24. Forecastle clamp
25. Iron hook over bowsprit
26. Forecastle waterway
27. Stem
28. Hawse hook
29. Hawse hole
30. Upper deck hook
31. Breast hook
32. Lower deck hook
33. Transom on the quarterdeck
34. Iron knee to the transom on the quarterdeck
35. Quarterdeck transom
36. Iron knee to the quarterdeck transom
37. Quarter gallery doorway
38. Seat transom
39. Iron knee to the seat transom
40. Upper deck waterway

41. Upper deck transom
42. Iron knee to the upper deck transom
43. Wing transom
44. Wooden knee to the wing transom
45. Diagonal transom knee
46. Lower deck waterway
47. Sleeper (pointer)
48. Crutch
49. Cabin scuttle
50. Combined iron standard and hanging knee
51. Upper deck clamp
52. Lower deck spirketting
53. Wooden standard
54. Orlop beam
55. Main mast step
56. Upper deck spirketting
57. Lower deck clamp
58. Air space
59. Fore mast step hooks
60. Fore mast step

C1/2

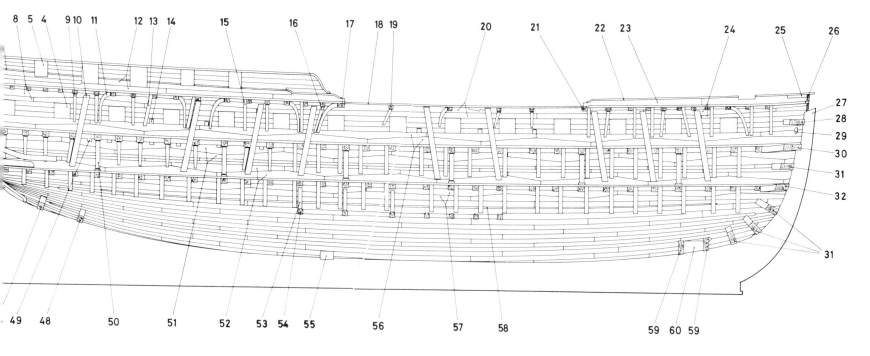

C Internal hull

C2/1

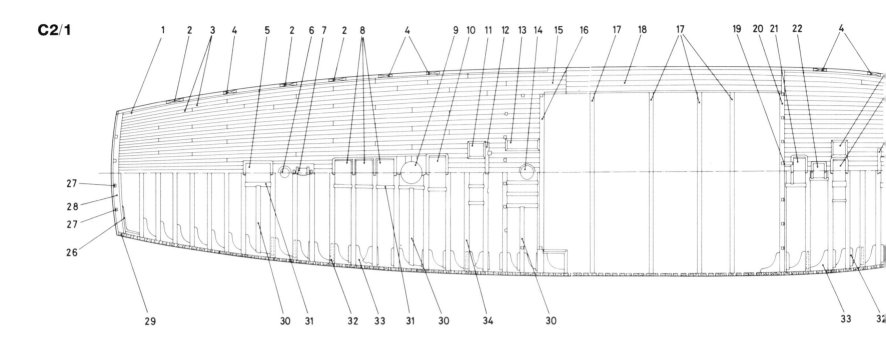

C2/2

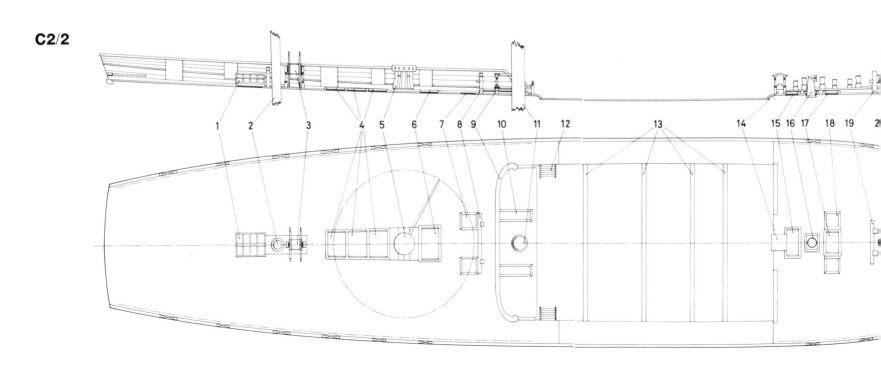

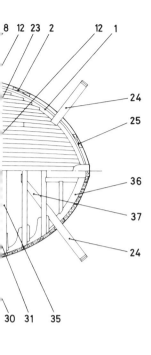

C2 QUARTERDECK AND FORECASTLE

C2/1 Plan of structure (1/192 scale)
1. Waterway
2. 32-pounder carronade port
3. Two oak strakes next to the waterway
4. 9-pounder gun port
5. Companion
6. Mizen mast
7. Wheel
8. Gratings
9. Capstan
10. Ladderway
11. Top-tackle scuttle
12. Bitts
13. Pump scuttle
14. Main mast
15. Fixed part of gangway
16. Quarterdeck breast beam
17. Skid beams
18. Gangway
19. Belfry stanchions
20. Forecastle breast beam
21. Steam grating
22. Funnel
23. Fore mast
24. Cathead
25. Chase port
26. Iron transom knee
27. Counter timber
28. Deck transom
29. Side counter timber
30. Half beam
31. Carling
32. Hanging knee
33. Lodging knee
34. Quarterdeck beam
35. Forecastle beam
36. Deck hook
37. Cat tail

C2/2 Arrangement of fittings (1/192 scale)
1. Companion
2. Mizen mast
3. Wheel
4. Gratings
5. Upper capstan
6. Ladderway
7. Main top-tackle scuttle
8. Brace bitts
9. Barricade
10. Pump scuttle
11. Main mast
12. Ladder
13. Skid beams
14. Belfry
15. Steam grating
16. Funnel
17. Grating
18. Fore top-tackle scuttle
19. Fore jeer bitts
20. Fore mast
21. Fore topsail sheet bitts
22. Cathead

C2/3 Belfry (left – after elevation; right – starboard elevation; 1/32 scale)
1. Canopy
2. Iron bell strap or crank
3. Bell beam
4. Bell
5. Stanchion

C2/3

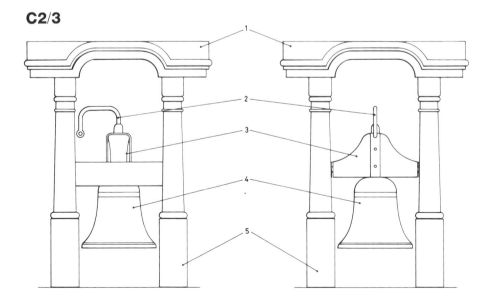

C3/1

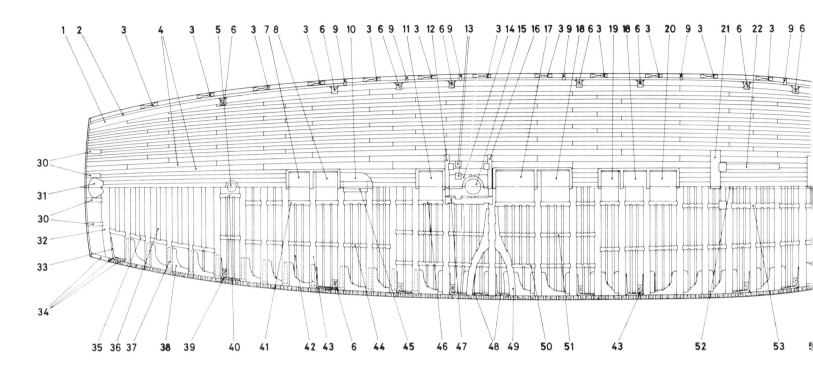

C3	**UPPER DECK**
C3/1	**Plan of structure (1/192 scale)**

1.	Waterway	29.	Stem
2.	Spirketting	30.	Counter timbers
3.	18-pounder gun port	31.	Helm port
4.	Binding strakes	32.	Deck transom
5.	Mizen mast	33.	Iron transom knee
6.	Top rider	34.	Side counter timber
7.	Companion	35.	Half beam carling
8.	Ladderway	36.	Half beam
9.	Scupper	37.	Iron hanging knee
10.	Capstan	38.	Lodging knee
11.	After hatchway	39.	Iron lodging knee in way of rider
12.	Main jeer bitts	40.	Mizen partners carling
13.	Pump	41.	Coaming carling
14.	Main mast chocks	42.	Ledge
15.	Main mast	43.	Beam
16.	Main topsail sheet bitts	44.	Carling
17.	Main hatchway	45.	Capstan step
18.	Ladderway	46.	Midship tier carlings
19.	Grating	47.	Main mast partner
20.	Fore hold	48.	Iron lodging knees
21.	Riding bitts	49.	Beam arm
22.	Standard	50.	Side tier carlings
23.	Fore mast chocks	51.	Middle tier carlings
24.	Fore mast	52.	Carling under the fire hearth
25.	Fore topsail sheet bitts	53.	Carling under the standard
26.	Bowsprit partners	54.	Fore jeer bitts, lower arm
27.	Bollard timber	55.	Fore mast partners
28.	Apron	56.	Ekeing
		57.	Deck hook
		58.	Hawse pieces

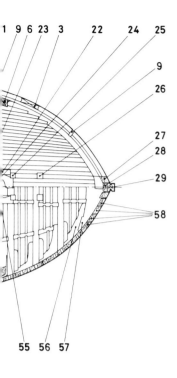

1 9 6 23 3   22   24   25

9

26

27

28

29

58

55 56 57

C3/2

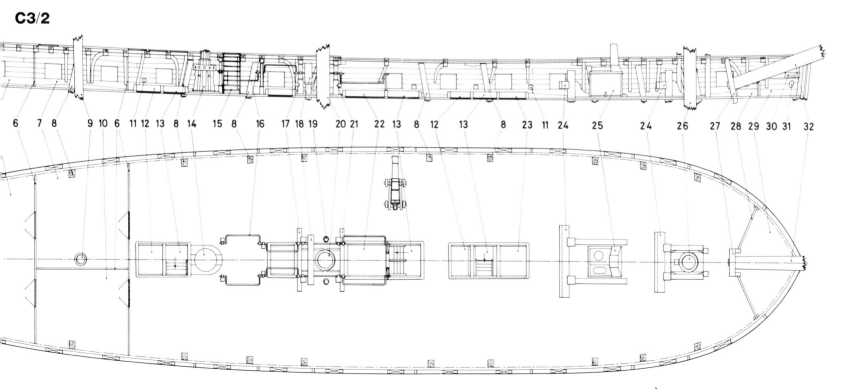

6 7 8   9 10 6 11 12 13 8 14 15 8 16 17 18 19 20 21 22 13 8 12 13   8 23 11 24   25   24   26   27 28 29 30 31 32

C Internal hull

C3/3 Galley Brodie stove – starboard side (1/24 scale)

1. Adjustable baffle plate
2. Swivelling funnel
3. Chain drive from smoke jack to spits
4. Lower spit
5. Oven door
6. Drip tray
7. Condenser delivery pipe
8. Condenser cooling water inlet
9. Condenser cooling water jacket
10. Condenser cooling water overflow
11. Boiler feed
12. Boiler lid
13. Ringbolt
14. Boiler
15. Flue access
16. Furnace firehole door
17. Ashpan door
18. Bottom plate
19. Stone tiles
20. Upper deck

C3/3

C3/4

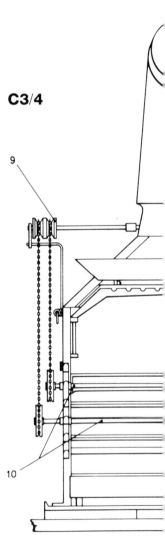

C3/4 Galley Brodie stove – fore side
(1/24 scale)
1. Swivelling funnel
2. Hinged flap
3. Swinging suspension arms
4. Ringbolt
5. Range grate
6. Drip pan
7. Stone tiles
8. Upper deck
9. Upper chain wheel of spit drive
10. Spits

C3/5 Galley Brodie stove – section
(1/24 scale)
1. Chimney
2. Impeller
3. Smoke jack
4. Gear box
5. Upper chain wheel
6. Swinging suspension arm
7. Flue
8. Oven
9. Drop bar
10. Front bars
11. Range grate
12. Drip tray
13. Condenser delivery pipe
14. Condenser cooling water inlet
15. Condenser cooling water jacket
16. Condenser cooling water overflow
17. Boiler feed
18. Boiler
19. Cock
20. Furnace
21. Bottom plate

C3/5

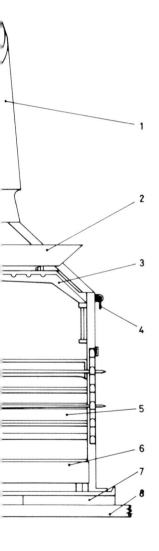

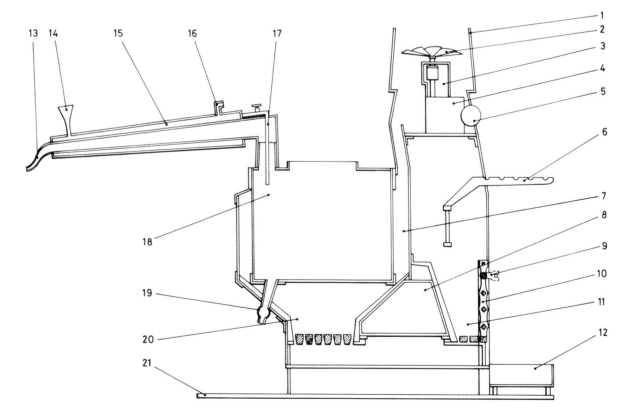

C4/1

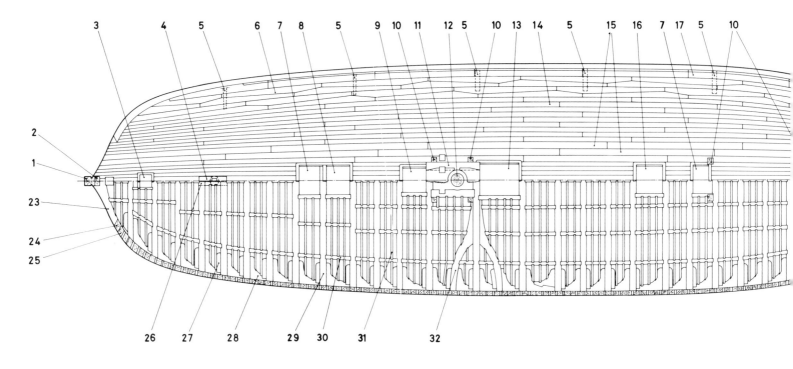

C4 LOWER DECK

C4/1 Plan of structure (1/192 scale)

1.	Stern post
2.	Inner post
3.	Scuttle to the bread room
4.	Mizen step
5.	Standard
6.	Four strakes of oak planking worked top and butt
7.	Ladderway
8.	Hatch to the fish room
9.	After hatch
10.	Bitt pin
11.	Main mast partners
12.	Main mast
13.	Main hatch
14.	Fir flat of deck
15.	Oak margin plank
16.	Fore hatch
17.	Waterway
18.	Fore partners
19.	Fore mast
20.	Stemson
21.	Apron
22.	Stem
23.	Deck transom
24.	After fashion piece
25.	Forward fashion piece
26.	Carling under the mizen step
27.	Hanging knee
28.	Lodging knee
29.	Beam
30.	Carling
31.	Ledge
32.	Beam arm
33.	Deck hook
34.	Hawse pieces

C4/2

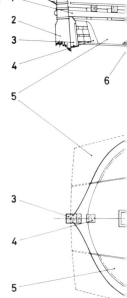

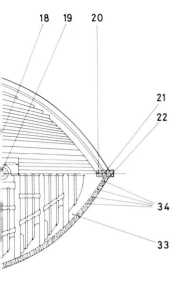

18 19 20

21
22

34

33

C4/2 Arrangement of fittings (1/192 scale)

1. Tiller
2. Rudder
3. Stern post
4. Sternson knee
5. Bread bins
6. Scuttle to the bread room
7. Mizen step
8. Mizen mast
9. Iron standard in cabins
10. Wardroom
11. Ladder down to the after platform
12. Ladder up
13. Wardroom bulkhead
14. Hatchway to the fish room
15. Captain's pantry
16. After hatchway
17. Pumps
18. Main mast
19. Main partners
20. Main hatchway

21. Ladder up to the waist
22. Top rider
23. Wooden standard
24. Ladder up to the waist
25. Fore hatchway
26. Ladder down to the fore platform
27. Bitt pin
28. Carling under the fire place
29. Hanging knee
30. Fore mast
31. Fore partner
32. Bowsprit step
33. Breasthook
34. Stem
35. Upper deck hook
36. Stemson
37. Apron
38. Line of the inner planking
39. Stemson
40. Stem
41. Apron

Cabins

A. Purser
B. Third Lieutenant
C. Master
D. Lieutenant of Marines
E. Captain's Clerk
F. Boatswain
G. Surgeon
H. First Lieutenant
I. Second Lieutenant
J. Captain of Marines
K. Gunner
L. Carpenter

35
36
37

8 9 10 11 12 13 14 9 15 16 17 18 19 20 21 22 23 24 25 26 27 28 29 27 30 31 32 33 34

A B C D E F

38

39

40

41

G H I J K L

C Internal hull

C5/1

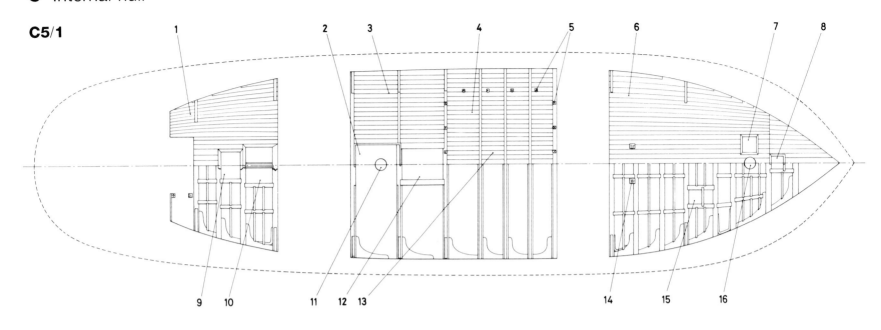

C5/2

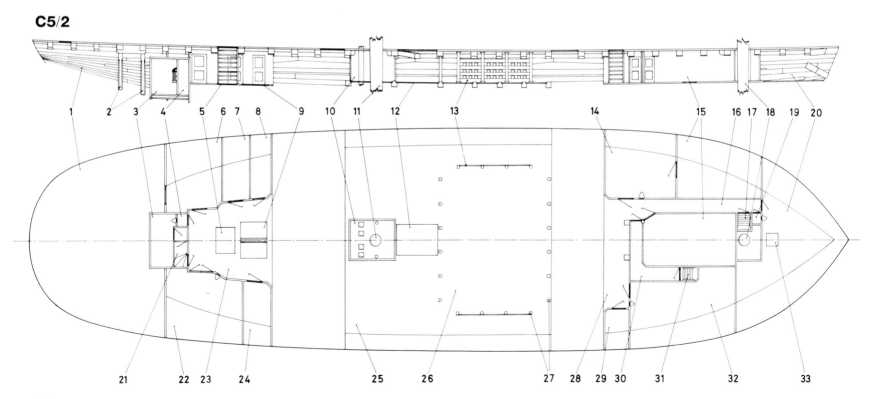

C5 ORLOP AND PLATFORMS

C5/1 Plan of structure (1/192 scale)
1. After platform
2. Well
3. Orlop
4. Cable tier
5. Cable tier stanchion
6. Fore platform
7. Scuttle to light room
8. Scuttle to fore peak
9. Fish room hatchway
10. Spirit room hatchway
11. Main mast
12. Main hatchway
13. Moveable planking
14. Riding bitt pins
15. Scuttle to fore magazine
16. Fore mast

C5/2 Arrangement of fittings (1/192 scale)
1. Bread room
2. Pillars to mizen mast step
3. After magazine
4. Light room
5. Fish room hatchway
6. Steward's room
7. Slop room
8. Marine clothing room
9. Spirit room hatchway
10. Well
11. Main mast
12. Main hatchway
13. Lattice bulkhead
14. Boatswain's store room
15. Sail room
16. Passage to gunner's store and light rooms
17. Ladder to magazine light room
18. Fore mast
19. Light room
20. Gunner's store
21. Passage to after magazine
22. Captain's store room
23. After platform (cockpit)
24. Lieutenant's store room
25. Orlop
26. Cable tier
27. Cable tier stanchions
28. Fore platform
29. Pitch room
30. Passage to fore magazine
31. Ladder to fore magazine
32. Carpenter's store room
33. Scuttle to fore peak

C6 HOLD

C6/1 Arrangement of fittings (1/192 scale)
1. Bread room
2. After magazine
3. Fish room
4. Spirit room
5. After hold
6. Shot locker
7. Chain pump
8. Main mast
9. Elm tree pump
10. Well
11. Main hold
12. Fore hold
13. Forward magazine
14. Filling room
15. Light room
16. Fore mast
17. Fore peak
18. Keelson

C6/1

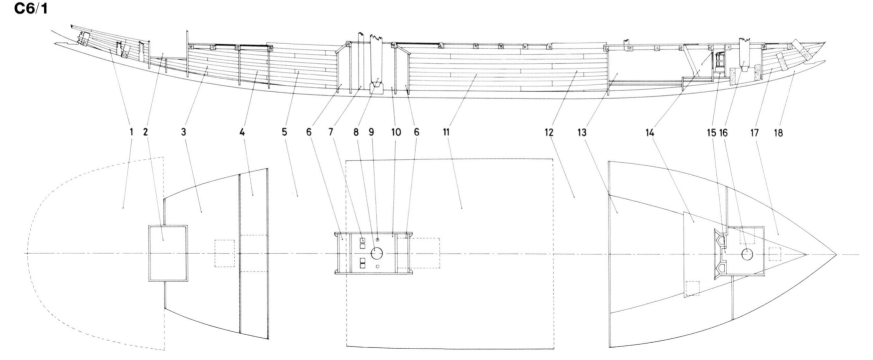

C Internal hull

C6/2 Stowage of iron ballast (1/96 scale)
1. Ground tier half pigs
2. Shot locker
3. Well
4. Main mast
5. Ground tier whole pigs
6. Line of floor heads
7. Keelson
8. Third tier
9. Second tier
10. Ballast cant

C6/2

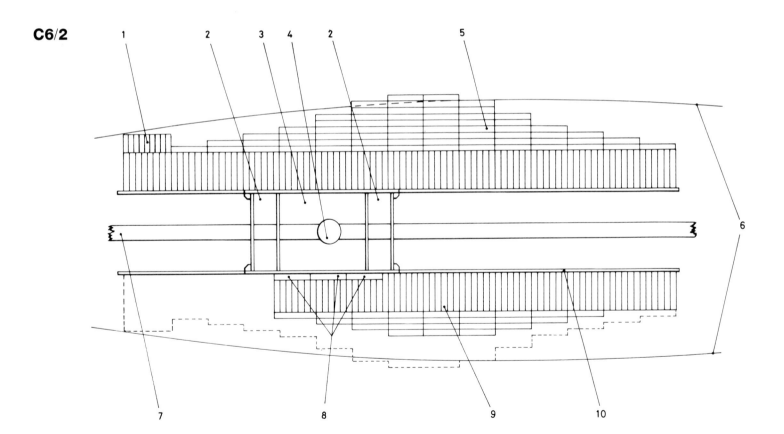

C6/3 Stowage of beer and water casks (starboard side – ground tier; larboard side – third tier; 1/96 scale)

1. Spirit room bulkhead
2. After hold
3. After edge of orlop
4. Keelson
5. Main hold
6. Orlop pillar
7. Forward edge of orlop
8. Fore hold
9. Forward magazine bulkhead
XX Section through main hold (see C6/5)
YY Section through fore hold (see C6/6)

C6/3

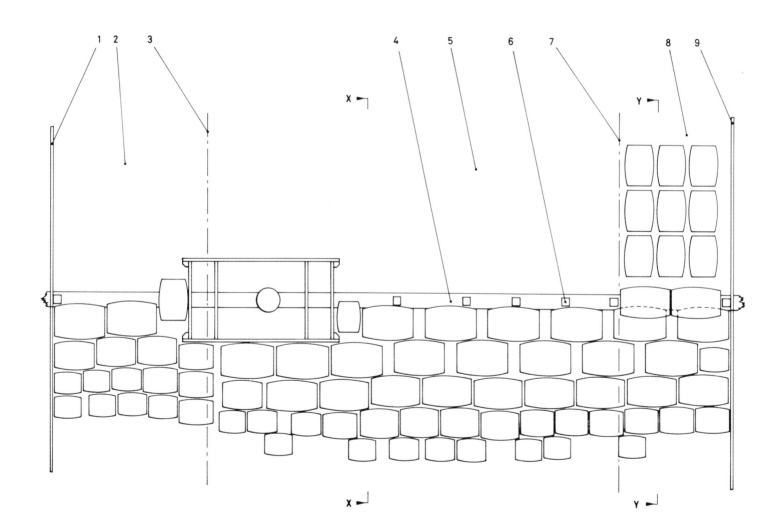

C6/4

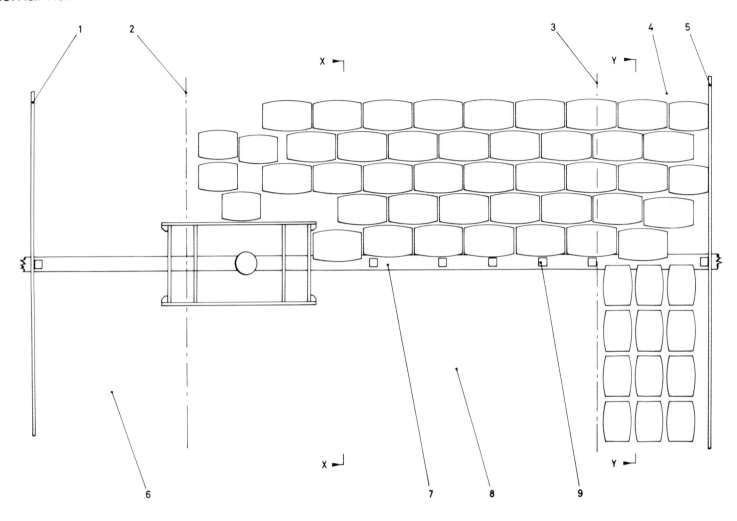

C6/5

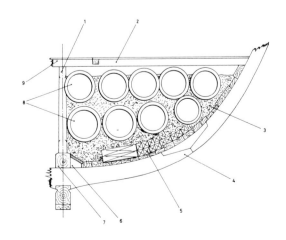

C6/6

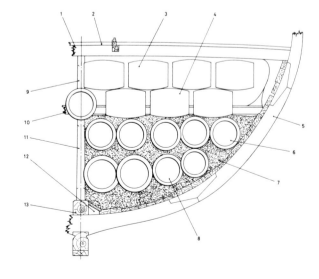

C6/4 Stowage of beer and water casks (larboard side – second tier; starboard side – fourth tier; 1/96 scale)

1. Spirit room bulkhead
2. After edge of orlop
3. Forward edge of orlop
4. Fore hold
5. Forward magazine bulkhead
6. After hold
7. Keelson
8. Main hold
9. Orlop pillar
XX Section through main hold (see C6/5)
YY Section through fore hold (see C6/6)

C6/5 Section through main hold looking forward (1/96 scale)

1. Orlop pillar
2. Orlop beam
3. Shingle ballast
4. Frame bend 3
5. Cast iron pig ballast
6. Limber passage
7. Keelson
8. Beer and water casks
9. Main hatchway

C6/6 Section through fore hold looking forward (1/96 scale)

1. Fore hatchway
2. Lower deck planking
3. Fourth tier of casks
4. Third tier of casks
5. Frame bend E
6. Second tier of casks
7. Shingle ballast
8. Ground tier of casks
9. Lower deck pillar
10. Orlop beam
11. Orlop pillar
12. Limber passage
13. Keelson

C6/7 Well and shot lockers (1/48 scale isometric)

1. Lower deck beams
2. Main mast
3. Loovered battens
4. Door – starboard side only
5. Corner stanchion
6. Orlop beam
7. Shot locker lid
8. Shot locker
9. Bulkhead
10. Keelson
11. Middle stanchion
12. Mast step
13. Syphered [bevel-edged] planking
14. Partition
15. Harris cut corner stanchion
16. Footwaling
17. Limber strakes
18. Limber passage
19. Limber board

C6/7

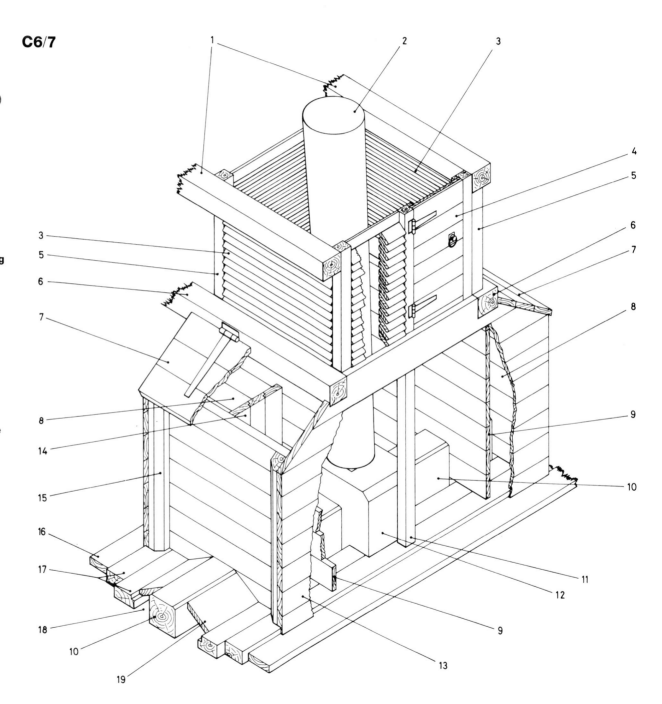

59

C Internal hull

C6/8

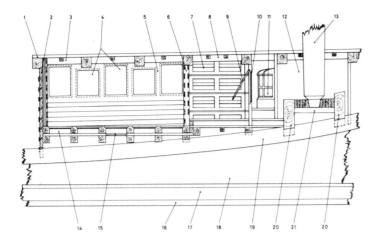

C6/9

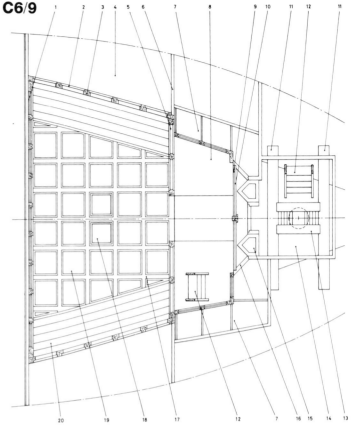

C6/8 Magazine and filling room, middle line section (1/96 scale)

1. Fore platform
2. Magazine bulkhead
3. Magazine
4. Wing panels
5. Wing stanchions
6. Battened bulkhead
7. Cartridge rack
8. Filling room
9. Hinged shutter
10. Hinged sash
11. Lantern
12. Light room
13. Fore mast
14. Palleting flat
15. Access scuttle to the limber
16. False keel
17. Keel
18. Deadwood
19. Keelson
20. Mast hook
21. Mast step

C6/10

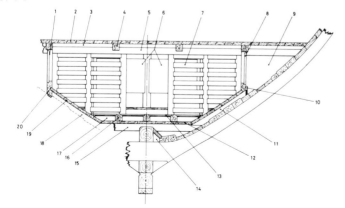

C6/9 Magazine and filling room, plan (1/96 scale)

1. Magazine bulkhead
2. Wing panel
3. Wing stanchion
4. Wing
5. Battened bulkhead
6. Water-tight bulkhead
7. Racks for cartridges
8. Filling room
9. Shutter
10. Light sash
11. Step hook
12. Ladder up
13. Mast step carling
14. Light room
15. Lantern
16. Spla board
17. Magazine
18. Access scuttle to limber
19. Palleting
20. Watercourse flat

C6/10 Section through the fore end of the magazine looking forward (1/96 scale)

1. Wing stanchion
2. Fore platform
3. Ledge
4. Carling
5. Beam
6. Shutters to sash lights
7. Battened bulkhead
8. Wing panel
9. Water-tight wing bulkhead
10. Perforated board
11. Watercourse chock
12. Magazine flat
13. Palleting
14. Limber passage
15. Magazine flat beam
16. Palleting carling
17. Palleting beam
18. Watercourse
19. Watercourse flat
20. Sill

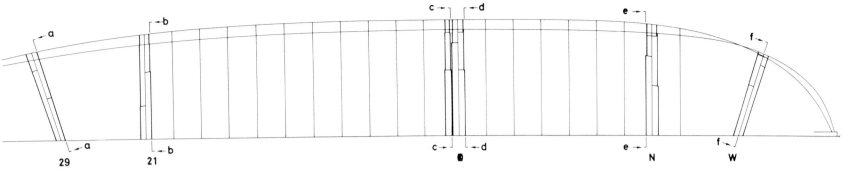

C7   SECTIONS

C7/1   Location plan of sections in C7/2
to C7/6 (1/192 scale)

- **aa**   Frame bend 29
- **bb**   Frame bend 21
- **cc**   Midship frame bend
- **dd**   Midship frame bend
- **ee**   Frame bend N
- **ff**   Frame bend W

C7/1

C7/2

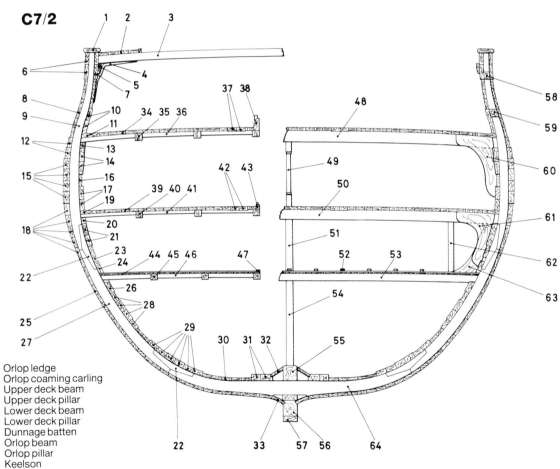

C7/2   Amidships (1/96 scale)

1. Gunwale
2. Gangboards
3. Skid beam
4. Skid beam iron knee
5. Skid beam clamp
6. Sheer strakes
7. String
8. Plank of the side
9. Fourth futtock
10. Upper deck spirketting
11. Upper deck waterway
12. Thickstuff on the wales
13. Filling piece
14. Upper deck clamps
15. Wales
16. Quickwork
17. Lower deck spirketting
18. Thickstuff under the wale and the
diminishing strakes
19. Lower deck waterway
20. Filling piece
21. Lower deck clamps
22. Filling chock
23. Air space
24. Strake on the end of the orlop beam
25. Plank of the bottom
26. Orlop clamp
27. Second futtock
28. Thickstuff on the first futtock head
29. Thickstuff on the floor head
30. Footwaling
31. Limber strakes
32. Limber board
33. Garboard strake
34. Upper deck plank
35. Upper deck carling
36. Upper deck ledge
37. Upper deck binding strakes
38. Upper deck hatch coaming carling
39. Lower deck plank
40. Lower deck carling
41. Lower deck ledge
42. Lower deck binding strakes
43. Lower deck coaming carling
44. Orlop plank
45. Orlop carling

46. Orlop ledge
47. Orlop coaming carling
48. Upper deck beam
49. Upper deck pillar
50. Lower deck beam
51. Lower deck pillar
52. Dunnage batten
53. Orlop beam
54. Orlop pillar
55. Keelson
56. Keel
57. False keel
58. Gun port upper sill
59. Gun port lower sill
60. Upper deck hanging knee
61. Lower deck hanging knee
62. Pillar
63. Orlop standard
64. Floor

C Internal hull

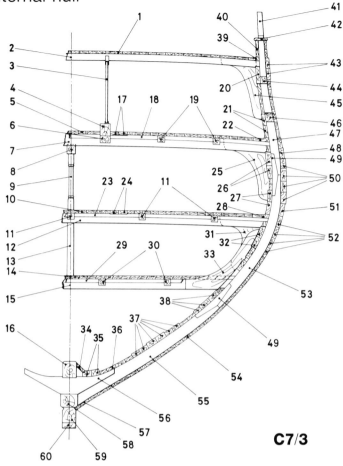

C7/3

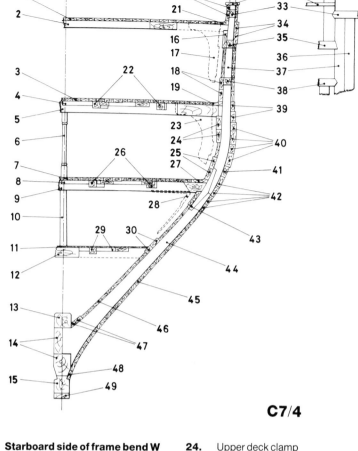

C7/4

	C7/3 Starboard side of frame bend N looking forward (1/96 scale)		
1.	Forecastle deck planking	**29.**	Fore platform ledge
2.	Forecastle beam	**30.**	Fore platform carling
3.	Iron pillar in way of fire place	**31.**	Lower deck hanging knee
4.	Standard to the after bitts	**32.**	Lower deck clamp
5.	Upper deck planking	**33.**	Fore platform standard
6.	Carling under the after bitt standard	**34.**	Limber board
7.	Upper deck beam	**35.**	Limber strakes
8.	Carling under the fire place	**36.**	Footwaling
9.	Upper deck pillar	**37.**	Thickstuff on the floor heads
10.	Lower deck planking	**38.**	Thickstuff on the first futtock heads
11.	Lower deck carlings	**39.**	Forecastle waterway
12.	Lower deck beam	**40.**	Forecastle spirketting
13.	Lower deck pillar	**41.**	Timberhead
14.	Fore platform plank rabbeted and caulked in way of the magazine	**42.**	Plansheer
15.	Fore platform beam	**43.**	Sheer strakes
16.	Keelson	**44.**	Upper port sill
17.	Upper deck binding strakes	**45.**	Forecastle hanging knee
18.	Upper deck ledge	**46.**	Lower port sill
19.	Upper deck carling	**47.**	Toptimber
20.	Forecastle clamp	**48.**	Thickstuff on the wales
21.	Upper deck spirketting	**49.**	Chock
22.	Upper deck waterway	**50.**	Wales
23.	Lower deck ledge	**51.**	Thickstuff under the wales
24.	Lower deck binding strakes	**52.**	Diminishing strakes
25.	Upper deck hanging knee	**53.**	Third futtock
26.	Upper deck clamp	**54.**	Plank of the bottom
27.	Lower deck spirketting	**55.**	First futtock
28.	Lower deck waterway	**56.**	Cross chock
		57.	Garboard strake
		58.	Rising wood
		59.	Keel
		60.	False keel

	C7/4 Starboard side of frame bend W looking forward (1/96 scale)		
1.	Forecastle deck planking	**24.**	Upper deck clamp
2.	Forecastle deck beam	**25.**	Lower deck spirketting
3.	Upper deck planking	**26.**	Lower deck carlings
4.	Upper deck ledge	**27.**	Lower deck waterway
5.	Upper deck beam	**28.**	Lower deck iron hanging knee
6.	Upper deck pillar	**29.**	Fore platform carlings
7.	Lower deck planking	**30.**	Thickstuff on the first futtock head
8.	Lower deck ledge	**31.**	Timberhead
9.	Lower deck beam	**32.**	Plansheer
10.	Lower deck pillar	**33.**	Carronade port sill
11.	Fore platform planking	**34.**	Sheer strakes
12.	Fore platform beam	**35.**	Upper sill of upper deck port
13.	Keelson	**36.**	Toptimber
14.	Deadwood	**37.**	Fourth futtock
15.	Keel	**38.**	Lower sill of upper deck port
16.	Forecastle clamp	**39.**	Thickstuff on the wales
17.	Forecastle hanging knee	**40.**	Wales
18.	Upper deck spirketting	**41.**	Thickstuff under the wales
19.	Upper deck waterway	**42.**	Diminishing strakes
20.	Forecastle spirketting	**43.**	Chock
21.	Forecastle waterway	**44.**	Second futtock
22.	Upper deck carlings	**45.**	Plank of the bottom
23.	Upper deck hanging knee	**46.**	Footwaling
		47.	Limber strakes
		48.	Garboard strake
		49.	False keel

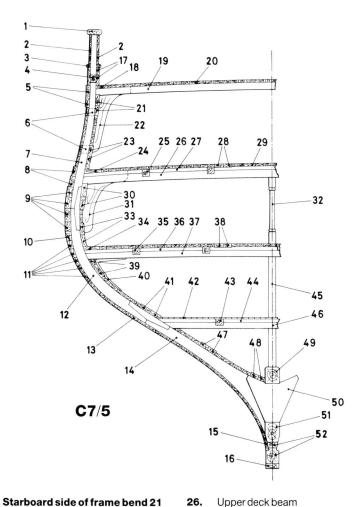

C7/5

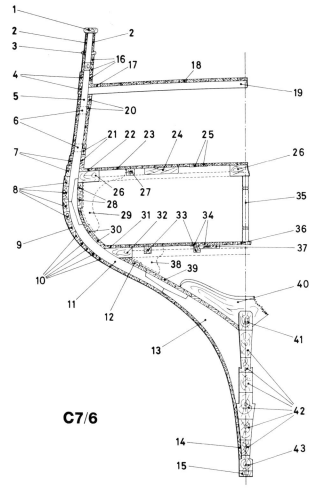

C7/6

C7/5	**Starboard side of frame bend 21 looking aft (1/96 scale)**	**26.**	Upper deck beam
		27.	Upper deck ledge
1.	Rough tree rail	**28.**	Upper deck binding strakes
2.	Berthing up	**29.**	Upper deck planking
3.	Plansheer	**30.**	Upper deck clamp
4.	Quarterdeck carronade port sill	**31.**	Upper deck hanging knee
5.	Sheer strakes	**32.**	Upper deck pillar
6.	Upper deck port sill	**33.**	Lower deck spirketting
7.	Toptimber	**34.**	Lower deck waterway
8.	Thickstuff on the wales	**35.**	Lower deck carling
9.	Wales	**36.**	Lower deck ledge
10.	Thickstuff under the wales	**37.**	Lower deck beam
11.	Diminishing strakes	**38.**	Lower deck binding strakes
12.	Third futtock	**39.**	Lower deck clamp
13.	Plank of the bottom	**40.**	Lower deck iron hanging knee
14.	First futtock	**41.**	Thickstuff on the first futtock head
15.	Garboard strake	**42.**	After platform planking
16.	False keel	**43.**	After platform carling
17.	Quarterdeck spirketting	**44.**	After platform ledge
18.	Quarterdeck waterway	**45.**	After platform pillar
19.	Quarterdeck beam	**46.**	After platform beam
20.	Quarterdeck planking	**47.**	Thickstuff on the floor heads
21.	Quarterdeck clamp	**48.**	Limber strakes
22.	Quarterdeck hanging knee	**49.**	Keelson
23.	Upper deck spirketting	**50.**	Cross chock
24.	Upper deck waterway	**51.**	Deadwood
25.	Upper deck carling	**52.**	Keel

C7/6	**Starboard side of frame bend 29 looking aft (1/96 scale)**	**21.**	Upper deck spirketting
		22.	Upper deck waterway
1.	Rough tree rail	**23.**	Upper deck planking
2.	Berthing up	**24.**	Upper deck half beam
3.	Plansheer	**25.**	Upper deck binding strakes
4.	Sheer strakes	**26.**	Upper deck beam
5.	Toptimber	**27.**	Upper deck carling
6.	Upper deck gun port sills	**28.**	Upper deck clamp
7.	Thickstuff on the wales	**29.**	Upper deck hanging knee
8.	Wales	**30.**	Lower deck spirketting
9.	Thickstuff under the wales	**31.**	Lower deck waterway
10.	Diminishing strakes	**32.**	Lower deck beam
11.	Third futtock	**33.**	Lower deck carlings
12.	Lower deck clamp	**34.**	Lower deck binding strakes
13.	First futtock	**35.**	Upper deck pillar
14.	Garboard strake	**36.**	Lower deck planking
15.	False keel	**37.**	Lower deck ledge
16.	Quarterdeck spirketting	**38.**	Lower deck hanging knee
17.	Quarterdeck waterway	**39.**	Ceiling
18.	Quarterdeck planking	**40.**	Crutch
19.	Quarterdeck beam	**41.**	Keelson
20.	Quarterdeck clamps	**42.**	Deadwood
		43.	Keel

C Internal hull

C8/1

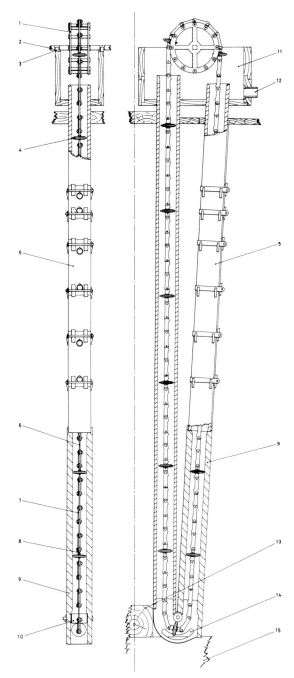

C8/2

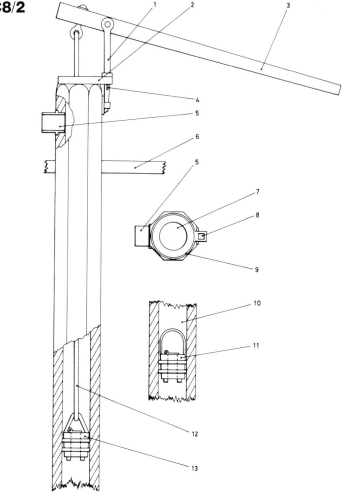

C8   PUMPS

C8/1 Chain pump (1/32 scale)
1.   Sprocket wheel
2.   Spindle
3.   Rhoding [bearing]
4.   Leather washer
5.   Square case
6.   Single link
7.   Double link
8.   Saucer link
9.   Cylindrical chamber
10. Cast iron roller
11. Cistern
12. Pump dale
13. Keelson
14. Water inlet
15. Floor

C8/2 Elm tree pump (1/24 scale)
1.   Forked stanchion
2.   Head hoop
3.   Brake
4.   Forelock
5.   Outlet (at right angles to brake)
6.   Upper deck
7.   Plan of head
8.   Socket for forked stanchion
9.   Head hoop
10. Section showing lower (fixed) valve
11. Fixed common box with valve
12. Operating rod
13. Moving common box with valve

C8/3

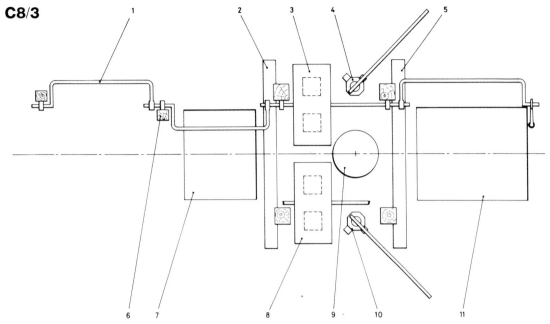

C8/3 Plan of upper deck (1/64 scale)
1. Chain pump brake
2. Main jeer bitts
3. Larboard chain pump cistern
4. Larboard elm tree pump
5. Main topsail sheet bitts
6. Stanchion
7. After hatchway
8. Starboard chain pump cistern
9. Main mast
10. Starboard elm tree pump
11. Main hatchway

C8/4

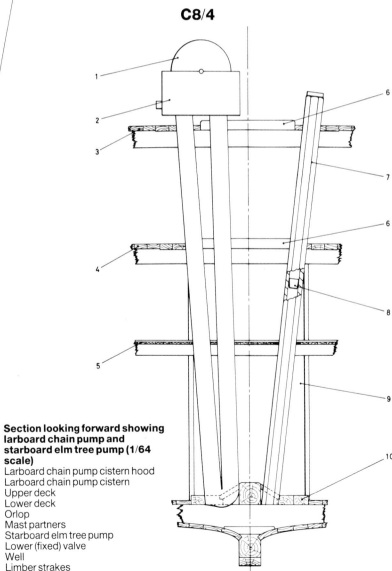

C8/4 Section looking forward showing larboard chain pump and starboard elm tree pump (1/64 scale)
1. Larboard chain pump cistern hood
2. Larboard chain pump cistern
3. Upper deck
4. Lower deck
5. Orlop
6. Mast partners
7. Starboard elm tree pump
8. Lower (fixed) valve
9. Well
10. Limber strakes

D External hull

D1/1

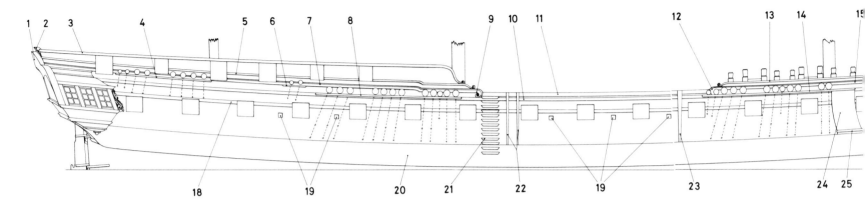

D   EXTERNAL HULL

D1   GENERAL

D1/1 Profile (1/192 scale)
 1. Taffarel
 2. Taffarel fife rail
 3. Rough tree rail
 4. Mizen channel
 5. Quarterdeck plansheer
 6. Backstay stool
 7. Quarterdeck drift rail
 8. Main channel
 9. Main drift
10. Sheer rail
11. Gunwale
12. Fore drift
13. Forecastle plansheer
14. Fore channel
15. Forecastle drift rail
16. Cat block
17. Cathead
18. Waist rail
19. Oar ports
20. Wale
21. Steps
22. Fenders
23. Chesstree
24. Anchor lining
25. Bolster
26. Head

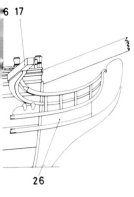

26

D1/2 Planking expansion (1/192 scale)
1. Rough tree rail
2. Quarterdeck plansheer
2. Quarterdeck berthing
4. Wale
5. Gunwale
6. Sheer strakes
7. Plank of the side
9. Thickstuff on the wale
9. Forecastle plansheer
10. Cathead
11. Hawse holes
12. Cheeks
13. Wale
14. Diminishing strakes
15. Plank of the bottom
16. Garboard strake

D1/2

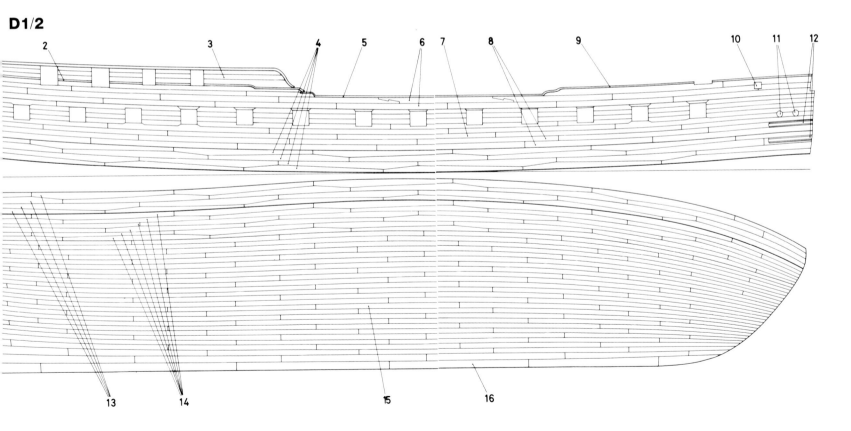

D External hull

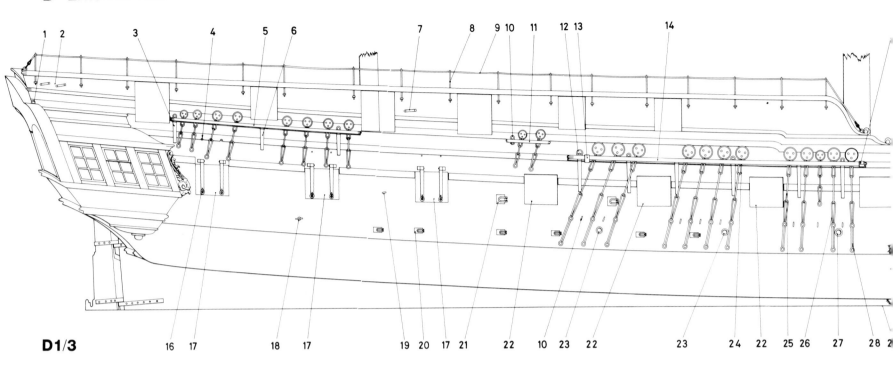

D1/3

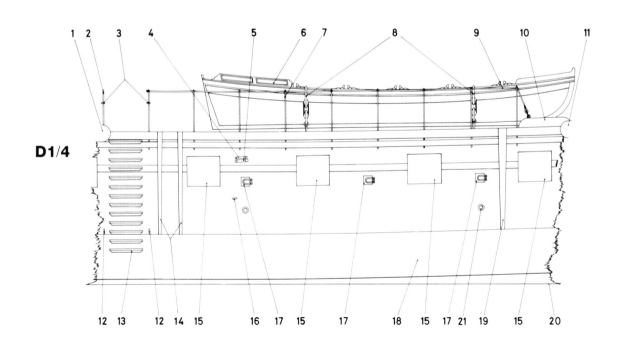

D1/4

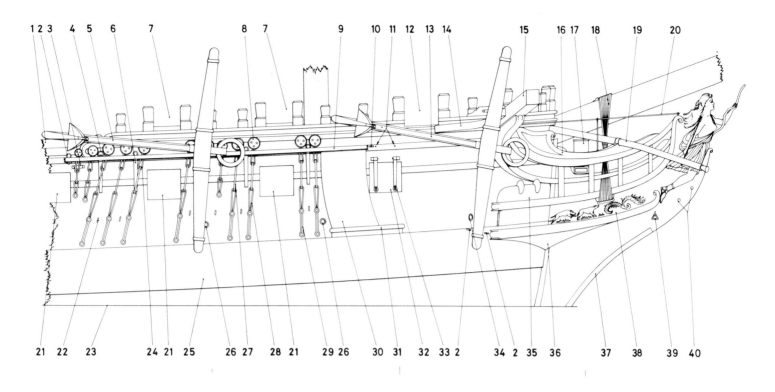

D1/5

1 2 3　4　5　6　7　8 7　9　10 11 12 13 14　15　16 17 18　19　20

21 22 23　24 21 25　26 27 28 21　29 26　30 31　32 33 2　34 2 35 36　37　38　39 40

D1/4　Waist details (1/96 scale)
1. Main drift
2. Gangway stanchion
3. Eye for entering rope
4. Fixed block for spritsail sheet
5. Fixed block for fore sheet
6. 32ft pinnace on the skid beams
7. Hammock netting crane
8. Gripes
9. Hammock netting ridge rope
10. Anchor bed
11. Fore drift
12. Eyebolt for entering rope
13. Steps
14. Fenders
15. Gun port without lid
16. Eyebolt for the standing end of the fore sheet
17. Oar port
18. Wale
19. Chesstree
20. Load waterline
21. 4in scupper

D1/5　Bow details (1/96 scale)
1. Anchor bed
2. Eyebolt
3. Fixed block for main tack
4. Swivel for shifting backstay
5. Spare bower anchor (starboard); sheet anchor (larboard)
6. Iron knee or tee plate with eyebolt
7. 9-pounder gun port
8. Deadeye
9. Fore channel
10. Eyebolt for fore lower studding sail boom gooseneck
11. Leaded hole for gun port lid tackle span
12. Carronade port
13. Best bower anchor (starboard); small bower anchor (larboard)
14. Cathead knee
15. Cathead
16. False rail
17. Seat of ease
18. Gammoning

19. Boomkin
20. Iron horse
21. Gun port without lid
22. Eyebolt
23. Load waterline
24. Upper link
25. Wale
26. 4in scupper
27. Middle link
28. Toe link
29. Preventer link
30. Anchor lining
31. Anchor lining bolster
32. Gun port with lid
33. Ringbolt for gun port lid tackle span
34. 5in manger scupper
35. Hawse bolster or navel hood
36. Wash cant
37. Lead sheathing to the gripe
38. Trailboard
39. Triangular ringbolt for the boomkin lashing
40. Holes for the bobstays

69

D External hull

D2 HEAD

D2/1 Starboard side from outboard (1/48 scale)

1. Forecastle plansheer
2. Cathead
3. Bollard timber
4. Horse
5. Seat of ease
6. False rail
7. Bowsprit
8. Block
9. Hair bracket
10. Lacing piece
11. Main rail
12. Lower rail
13. Bobstay piece
14. Forward head timber
15. Middle head timber
16. Gammoning bolster
17. Gammoning slot
18. After head timber
19. Stem timber
20. Trailboard
21. Cathead supporter
22. Ekeing
23. Hawse holes
24. Bolster
25. Upper cheek
26. Filling piece
27. Lower cheek
28. Wash cant

D2/1

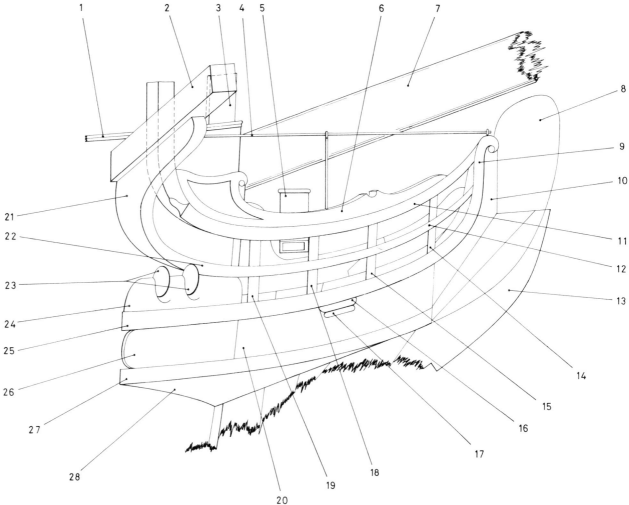

D2/2

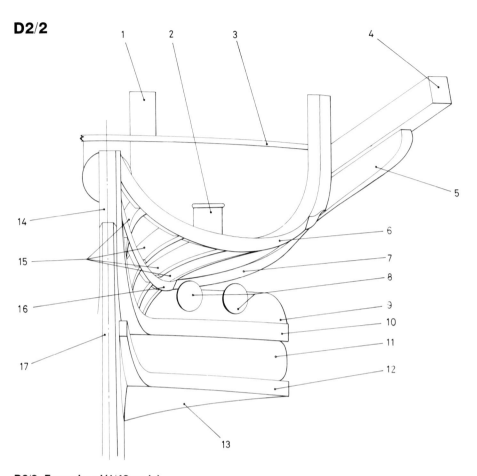

D2/2 From ahead (1/48 scale)
1. Bollard timber
2. Seat of ease
3. Forecastle plansheer
4. Cathead
5. Cathead supporter
6. Main rail
7. Ekeing
8. Hawseholes
9. Bolster
10. Upper cheek
11. Filling piece
12. Lower cheek
13. Wash cant
14. Lacing piece
15. Head timber
16. Lower rail
17. Bobstay piece

D2/3 Larboard side from inboard (1/48 scale)
1. Stem
2. After cross piece
3. Seat of ease
4. Ledge
5. False rail
6. Middle cross piece
7. Carling
8. Forward cross piece
9. Main rail
10. Lacing piece
11. Head timbers
12. Gammoning slot
13. Gammoning knee (standard)
14. Hole for mainstay collar

D2/3

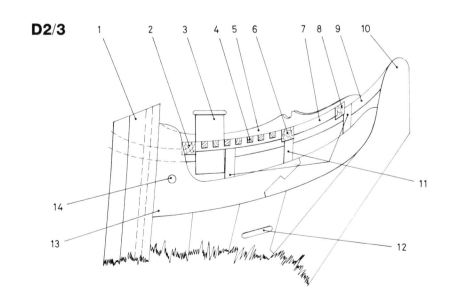

D External hull

D2/4 Plan with gratings (1/48 scale)

1. Cathead
2. Main rail
3. False rail
4. Ledges
5. After cross piece
6. Seat of ease
7. Ledges
8. Middle cross piece
9. Forward cross piece
10. Lacing
11. Chock
12. Bobstay piece
13. Carlings
14. Gammoning knee
15. Stem
16. Apron

D2/4

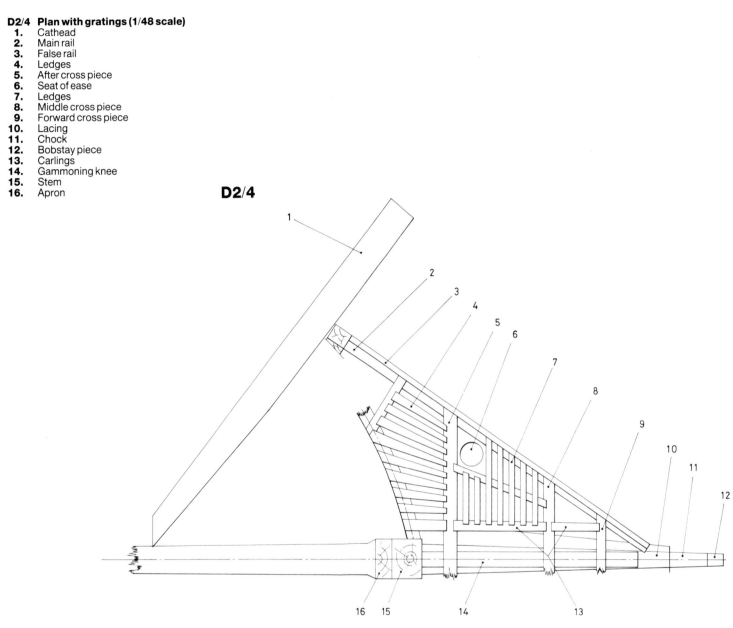

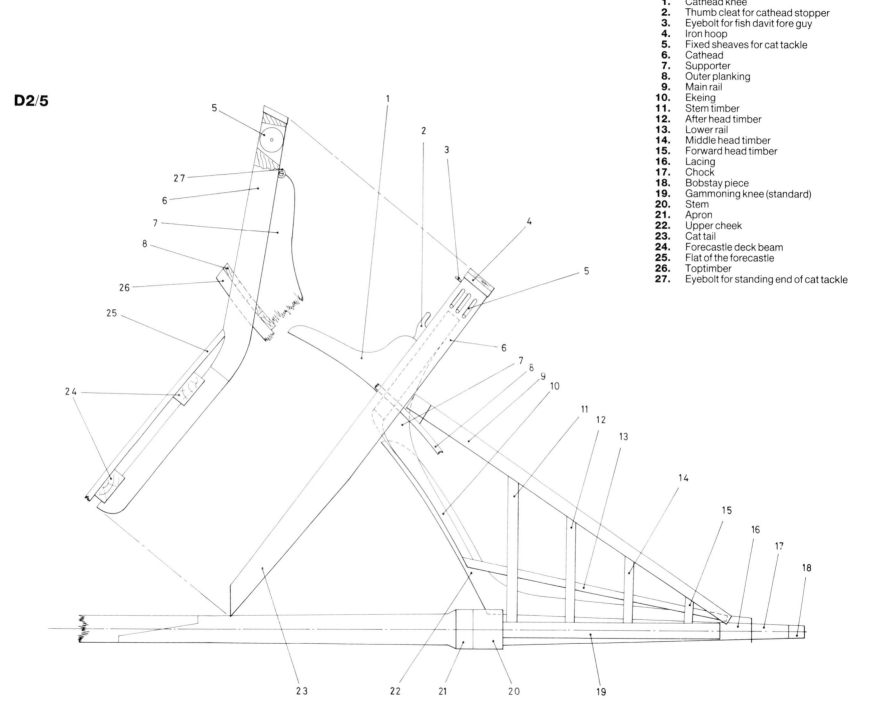

D2/5

D2/6

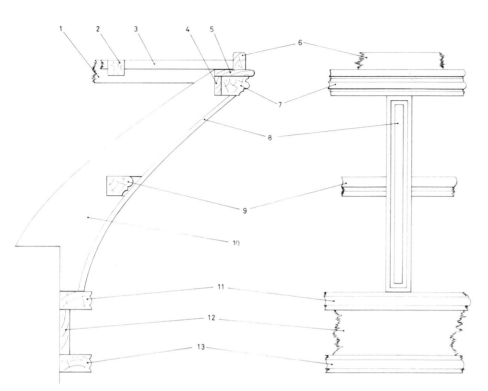

D2/8

D2/7

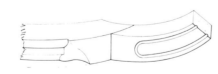

D2/6 Rails, diagrammatic (no scale)
1. Cross piece
2. Carling
3. Ledge
4. Inner lining
5. Plansheer (upper lining)
6. False rail
7. Main rail
8. Face piece
9. Lower rail
10. Head timber
11. Upper cheek
12. Filling piece
13. Lower cheek

D2/7 Moulding details (left – part of the larboard main rail; right – part of the starboard middle rail and ekeing; no scale)

D2/8 Figurehead (1/32 scale)

E Anchors and cables

E1 ARRANGEMENT

E1/1 Profile (messenger rigged to heave in on starboard cable; 1/192 scale)

1. Quarterdeck
2. Upper deck
3. Lower capstan
4. Upper capstan
5. Main hatchway
6. Overhead roller
7. Returning messenger
8. Riding bitts
9. Forecastle
10. Vertical roller
11. Starboard inner hawse hole
12. Bowsprit
13. Mizen mast
14. Lower deck
15. Heaving side of messenger
16. Main mast
17. Compressor
18. Cable tier
19. Orlop
20. Fore mast
21. Starboard cable

E1/2 Upper deck plan (ship riding to larboard anchor; messenger rigged to heave in on starboard cable; 1/192 scale)

1. Mizen mast
2. Capstan
3. After hatchway
4. Main mast
5. Main hatchway
6. Deck stopper
7. Fore hatchway
8. Larboard cable bitted
9. Bitt stopper
10. Fore mast
11. Manger
12. Hawse holes
13. Messenger
14. Roller
15. Compressor
16. Starboard cable nipped to messenger ready to heave in
17. Riding bitts

E1/1

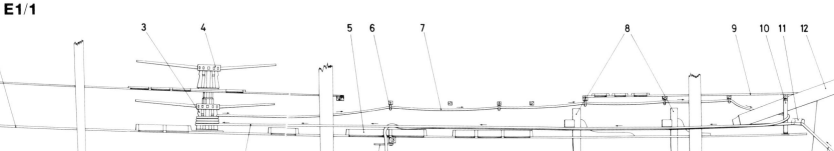
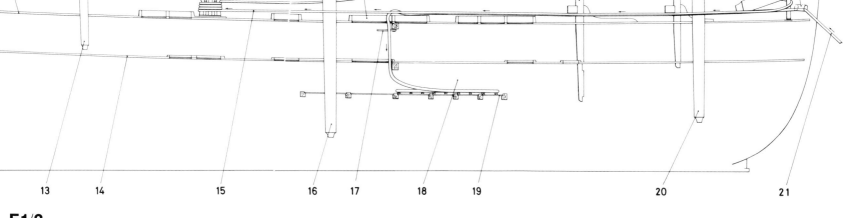

E1/2

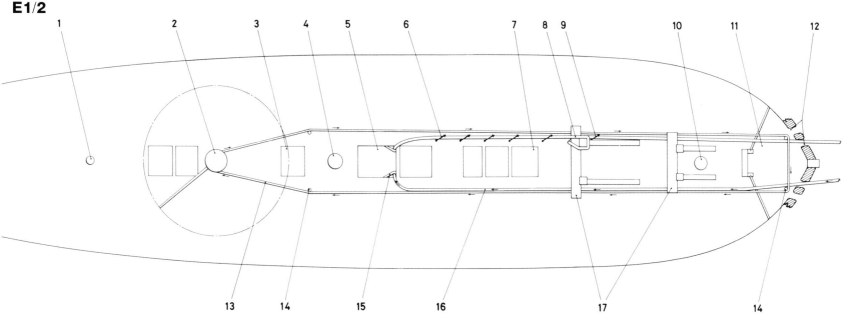

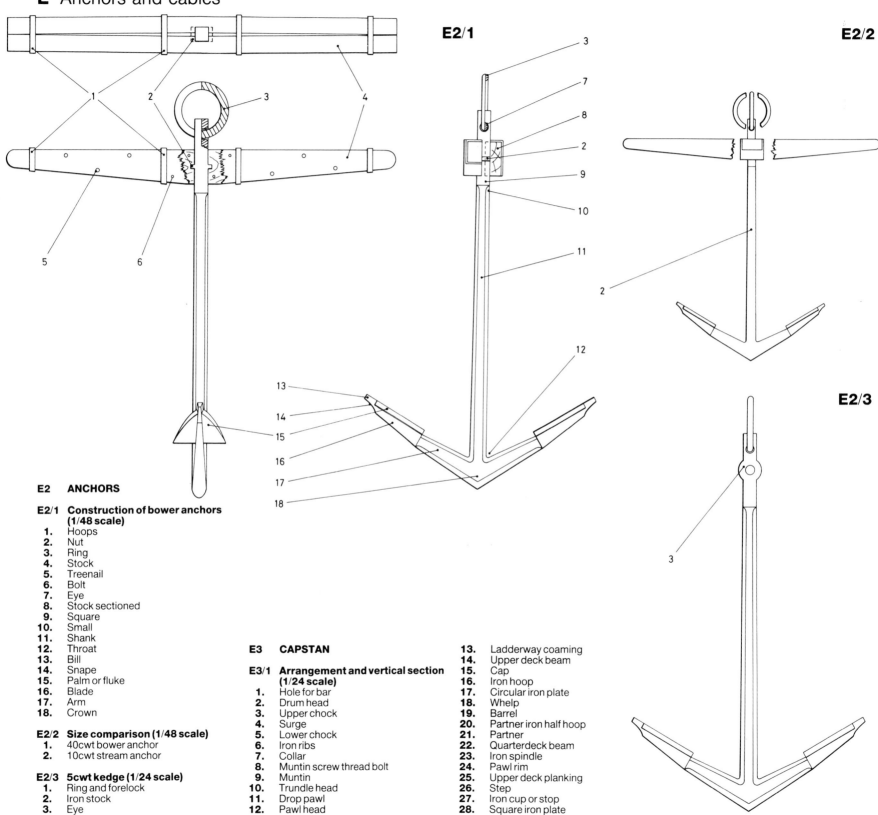

E2/1

E2/2

E2/3

E2   ANCHORS

**E2/1   Construction of bower anchors
(1/48 scale)**
1. Hoops
2. Nut
3. Ring
4. Stock
5. Treenail
6. Bolt
7. Eye
8. Stock sectioned
9. Square
10. Small
11. Shank
12. Throat
13. Bill
14. Snape
15. Palm or fluke
16. Blade
17. Arm
18. Crown

E2/2   Size comparison (1/48 scale)
1. 40cwt bower anchor
2. 10cwt stream anchor

E2/3   5cwt kedge (1/24 scale)
1. Ring and forelock
2. Iron stock
3. Eye

E3   CAPSTAN

**E3/1   Arrangement and vertical section
(1/24 scale)**
1. Hole for bar
2. Drum head
3. Upper chock
4. Surge
5. Lower chock
6. Iron ribs
7. Collar
8. Muntin screw thread bolt
9. Muntin
10. Trundle head
11. Drop pawl
12. Pawl head

13. Ladderway coaming
14. Upper deck beam
15. Cap
16. Iron hoop
17. Circular iron plate
18. Whelp
19. Barrel
20. Partner iron half hoop
21. Partner
22. Quarterdeck beam
23. Iron spindle
24. Pawl rim
25. Upper deck planking
26. Step
27. Iron cup or stop
28. Square iron plate

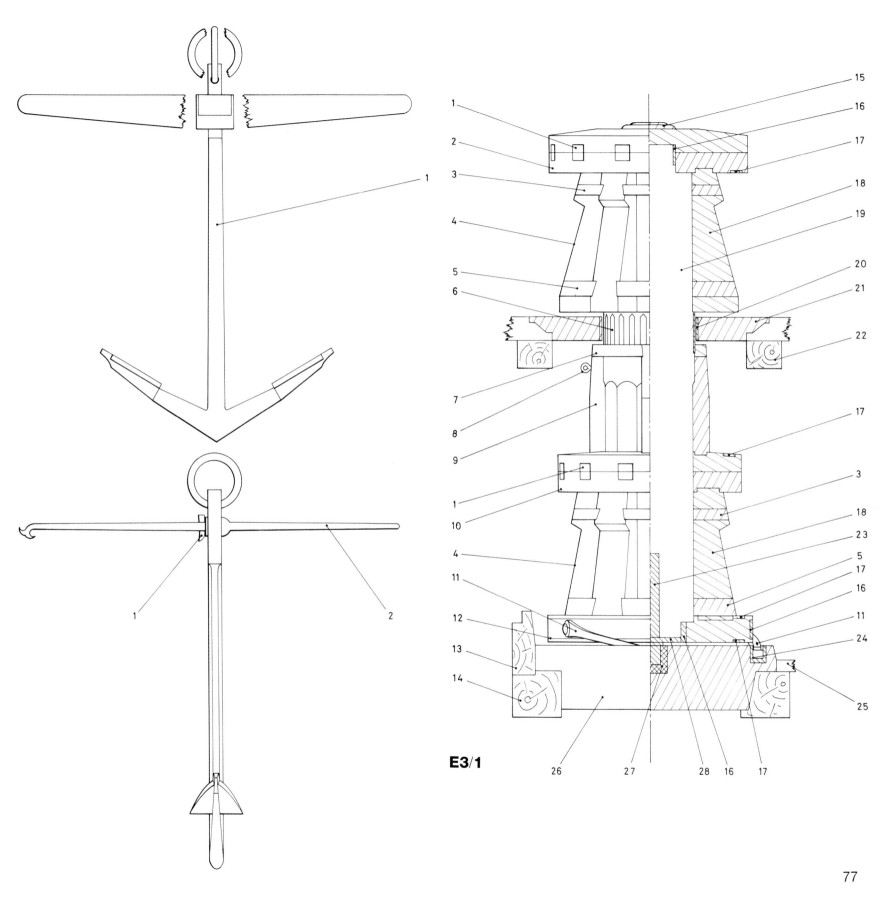

E3/1

F Spars and rigging

F1   **SPARS**

F1/1   **Spar plan (1/384 scale)**
1. Mizen royal yard
2. Long pole head to mizen topgallant mast
3. Mizen topgallant yard
4. Mizen topgallant mast
5. Mizen topsail yard
6. Mizen topmast
7. Gaff
8. Crossjack
9. Mizen mast
10. Ensign staff
11. Driver boom
12. Main royal yard
13. Long pole head to main topgallant mast
14. Main topgallant yard
15. Main topgallant mast
16. Main topsail yard
17. Main topmast
18. Main yard
19. Main mast
20. Fore royal yard
21. Long pole head to fore topgallant mast
22. Fore topgallant yard
23. Fore topgallant mast
24. Fore topsail yard
25. Fore topmast
26. Fore yard
27. Fore mast
28. Bowsprit
29. Jibboom
30. Jack staff
31. Spritsail yard

F1/2

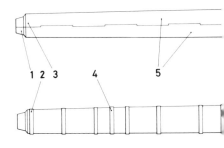

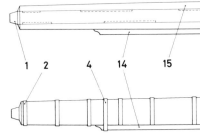

F1/1

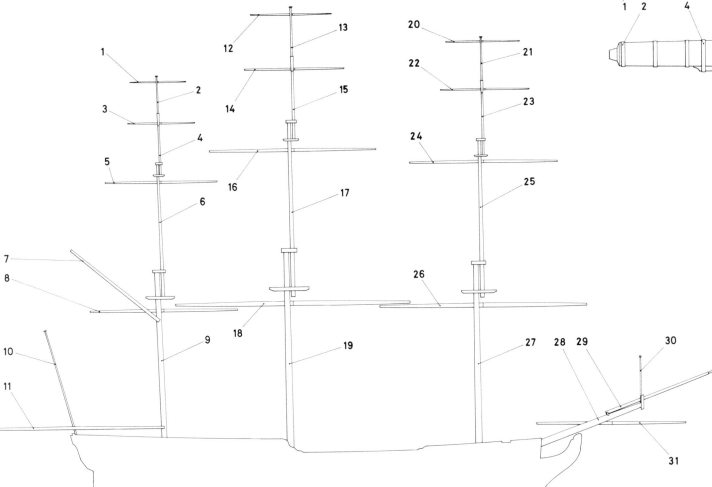

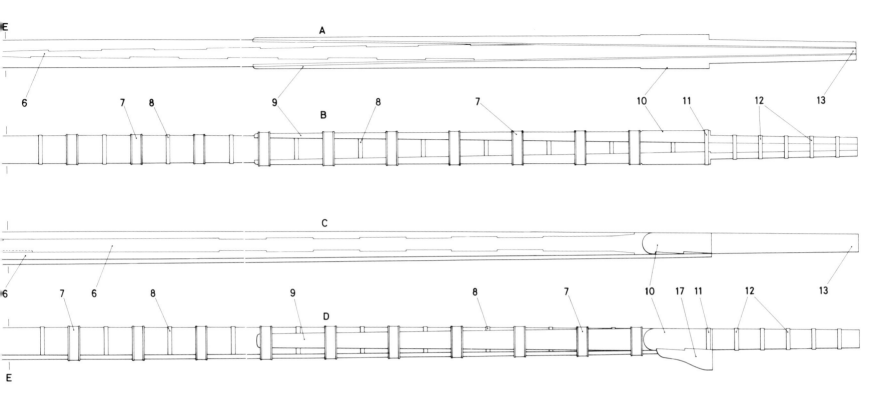

F1/2 Main mast (1/96 scale)

- **A.** Athwartships – construction
- **B.** Athwartships – arrangement from aft
- **C.** Fore and aft – construction
- **D.** Fore and aft – arrangement from starboard
- **E.** Line of partners at upper deck
- **1.** Heel tenon
- **2.** Heel hoop
- **3.** Heel
- **4.** Fish hoop
- **5.** Side trees
- **6.** Spindle
- **7.** Woolding
- **8.** Iron hoop
- **9.** Cheek
- **10.** Hounds
- **11.** Cheek hoop
- **12.** Head hoops
- **13.** Head
- **14.** Front fish
- **15.** After side fish
- **16.** Forward side fish
- **17.** Bib

F Spars and rigging

F1/3 Lower masts – size comparison (1/192 scale)

1. Made main mast
2. Made fore mast
3. Single tree mizen mast
4. Line of partners at upper deck

F1/3

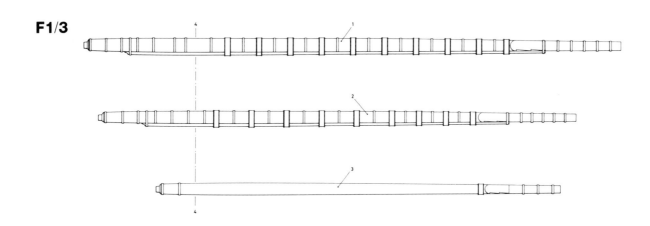

F1/4 Topmasts (1/96 scale)

1.	Lower sheave hole for the top rope	9.	Main topmast – after side
2.	Fid hole	10.	Circular section
3.	Upper sheave hole for the top rope	11.	Hounds – eight-square section
4.	Main topmast – larboard side	12.	Stop
5.	Hoop	13.	Head – square section
6.	Block – eight-square section	14.	Cheek block
7.	Heeling – square section	15.	Cap tenon
8.	Eight-square section	16.	Fore topmast
		17.	Mizen topmast

F1/4

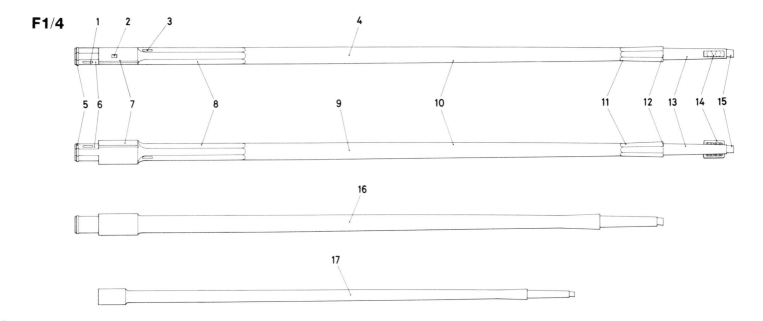

F1/5 Topgallant masts (1/96 scale)

1. Main topgallant mast – after side
2. Stump pole head
3. Common pole head
4. Long pole head
5. Heel – square section
6. Sheave hole for the top rope
7. Sheave hole for the topsail tye
8. Sheave hole for the staysail halliard
9. Truck
10. Sheave hole for the flag or royal halliard
11. Main topgallant mast – larboard side
12. Hounds – eight-square section
13. Stop
14. Fore topgallant mast
15. Mizen topgallant mast

F1/5

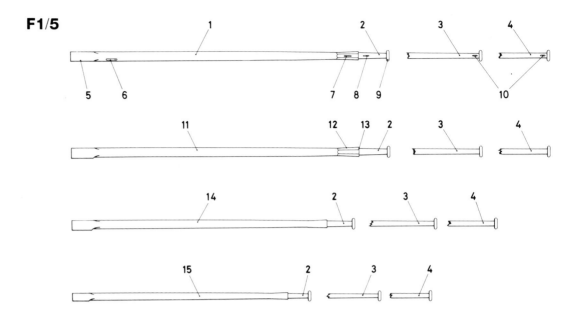

F1/6 Main top (1/96 scale)

A. Section from starboard
B. From ahead
C. Plan

1. Battens
2. Rail
3. Stanchion
4. Gunwale
5. Timber
6. Bolster
7. Cross tree
8. Main topmast
9. Cap
10. Eyebolts
11. Chock
12. Rim
13. Deals
14. Trestle tree
15. Fid
16. Bib
17. Main mast
18. Filling
19. Fid plate
20. Swivel socket plate
21. Slot for futtock plate

F1/6

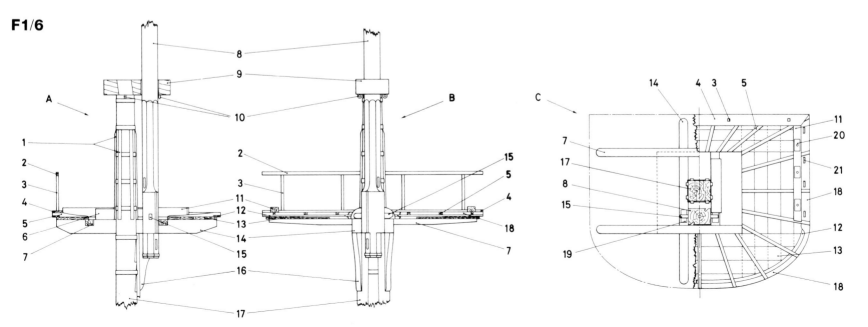

F Spars and rigging

F1/7

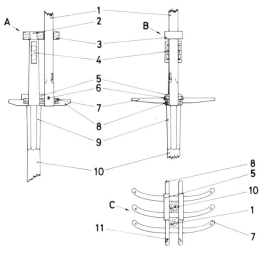

F1/8

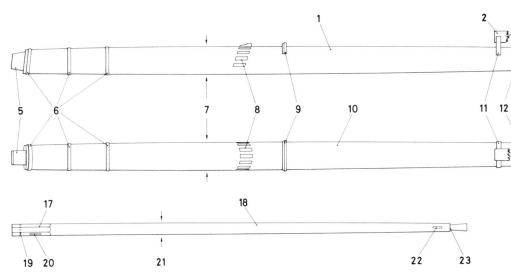

F1/7 Main topmast cross trees (1/96 scale)

A.	Section from starboard
B.	From ahead
C.	Plan
1.	Main topgallant mast
2.	Tenon
3.	Cap
4.	Cheek blocks
5.	Bolster
6.	Fid
7.	Cross tree
8.	Trestle tree
9.	Hounds
10.	Main topmast
11.	Sheave for fore topgallant brace

F1/8 Bowsprit and jibboom (1/96 scale)

1.	Bowsprit – starboard side
2.	Jibboom heel
3.	Bee's seat
4.	Bee block
5.	Heel tenon
6.	Hoops
7.	Bed
8.	Position of the gammoning cleats
9.	Fairlead saddle
10.	Bowsprit – plan
11.	Jibboom saddle
12.	Spritsail sling saddle
13.	Woolding
14.	Larboard bee
15.	Square
16.	Cap tenon
17.	Heel – eight-square section
18.	Jibboom plan
19.	Hole for heel lashing
20.	Sheave hole for the top rope
21.	Cap
22.	Sheave for the outhauler
23.	Stop

F1/9 Bowsprit cap (1/48 scale)

1.	Hole for the heel lashing
2.	Sheave hole for the top rope
3.	Eight-square section
4.	Jibboom
5.	Jack staff
6.	Leathered hole for the jibboom
7.	Starboard bee
8.	Sheave for the fore topmast stay
9.	Section on AA looking forward
10.	Bowsprit
11.	Jibboom saddle
12.	Spritsail sling saddle
13.	Woolding
14.	Starboard bee
15.	Bee block
16.	Sheave for the fore topmast preventer stay – larboard side
17.	Sheave for the fore topmast stay – starboard side
18.	Square
19.	Cap
20.	Forelock
21.	Bolt

F1/9

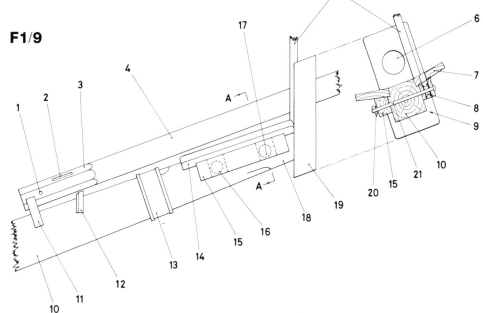

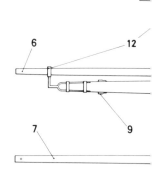

F1/11

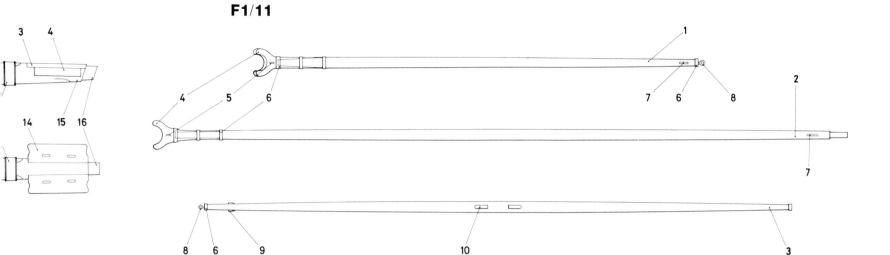

F1/10 Main yards and studding sail booms (1/96 scale)

1. Royal yard – plan
2. Topgallant yard – plan
3. Topsail yard – plan
4. Lower yard – plan
5. Topgallant studding sail boom – plan
6. Top studding sail boom – plan
7. Lower studding sail boom – elevation

8. Hoop
9. Stop cleat
10. Sling cleat
11. Sprig eyebolt
12. Outer boom iron
13. Inner (hinged) boom iron
14. Eight-square section
15. Battens
16. Gooseneck

F1/11 Driver boom, gaff and spritsail yard (1/96 scale)

1. Gaff – plan
2. Driver boom – plan
3. Spritsail yard from below
4. Jaws
5. Eyebolt
6. Hoop
7. Sheave hole
8. Sprig eyebolt
9. Stop cleat
10. Sling cleat

F1/10

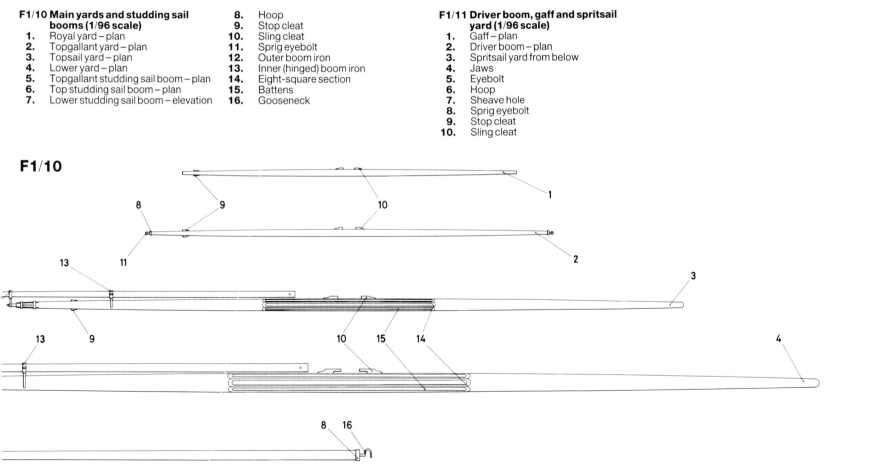

F Spars and rigging

F2/1

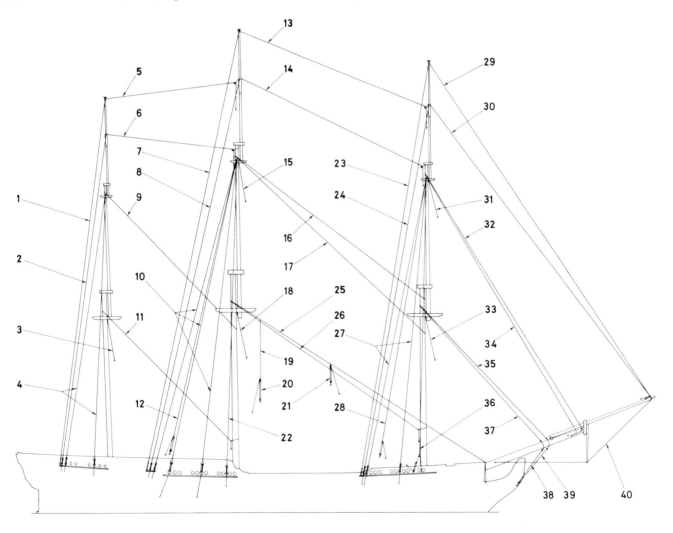

F2/2

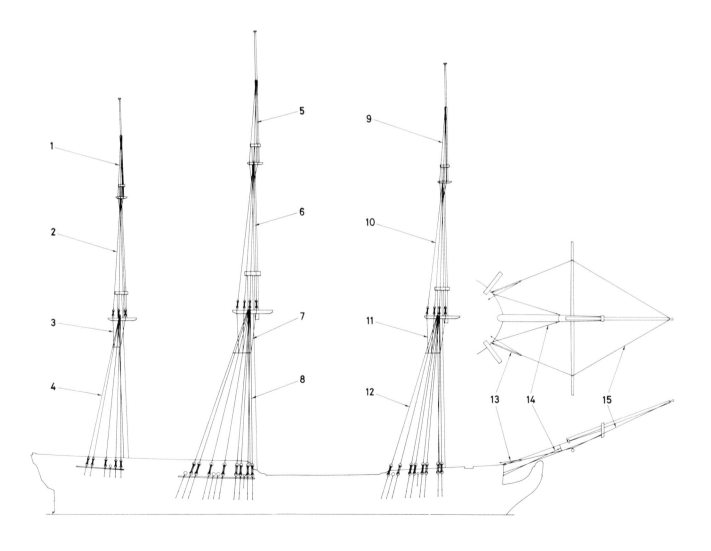

F Spars and rigging

F2/3

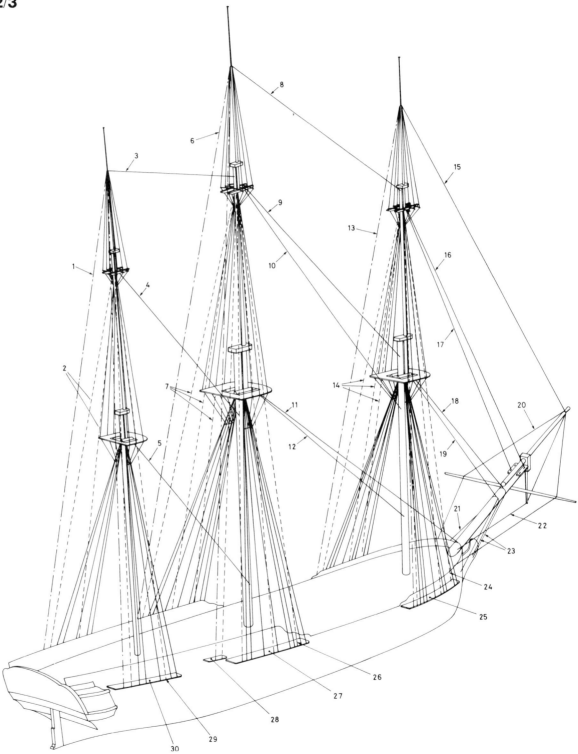

F3   SAILS

F3/1   Sail plan – square sails (1/384 scale)

1. Mizen royal
2. Mizen topgallant
3. Mizen topsail
4. Main royal
5. Main topgallant
6. Main topsail
7. Main course
8. Fore royal
9. Fore topgallant
10. Fore topsail
11. Fore course
12. Spritsail

F3/1

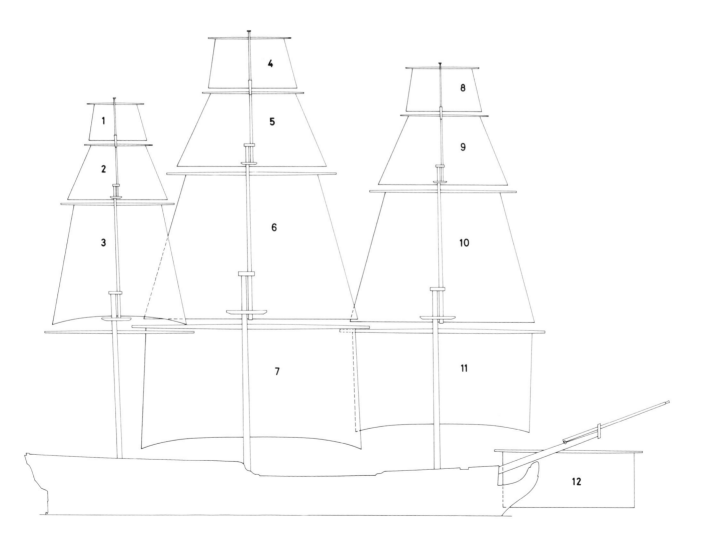

F Spars and rigging

F3/2 Sail plan – fore and aft sails (1/384 scale)

1. Driver
2. Mizen topgallant stay
3. Mizen topmast stay
4. Mizen staysail stay
5. Mizen topgallant staysail
6. Mizen topmast staysail
7. Mizen staysail
8. Main topgallant staysail stay
9. Middle staysail stay
10. Main topmast preventer stay
11. Main staysail stay
12. Main topgallant staysail
13. Middle staysail
14. Main topmast staysail
15. Main staysail
16. Jib stay
17. Fore topmast preventer stay
18. Fore preventer stay
19. Jib
20. Fore topmast staysail
21. Fore staysail

F3/3 Courses – fore side (1/192 scale)

1. Earing
2. Main course
3. Reef bands
4. Head bolt rope
5. Outline of fore course
6. Clue rope
7. Tabling
8. Bunt line cloth
9. Bunt line cringle
10. Middle band
11. Foot bolt rope
12. Lining
13. Upper reef cringle
14. Lower reef cringle
15. Upper bowline cringle
16. Middle bowline cringle
17. Lower bowline cringle
18. Leech bolt rope

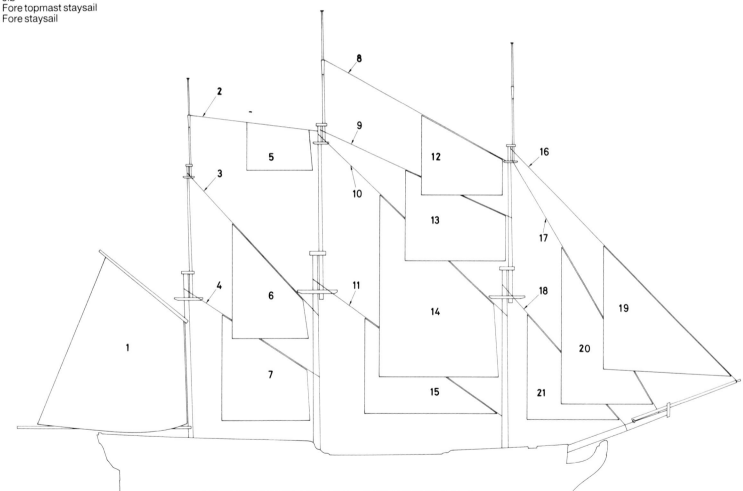

F3/3

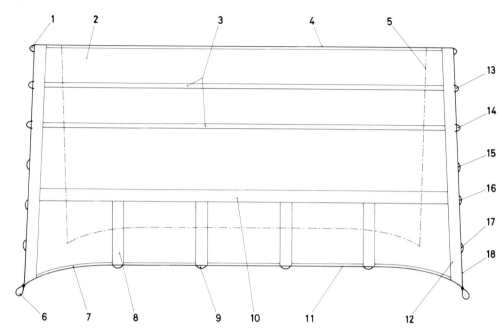

F3/4

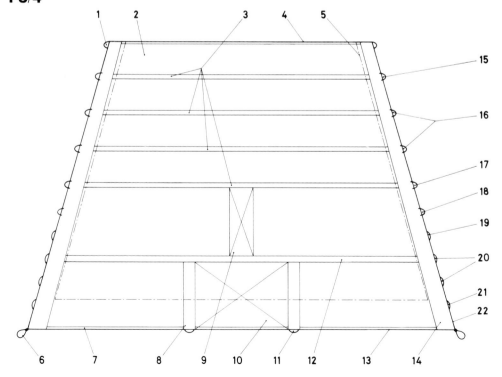

F3/5

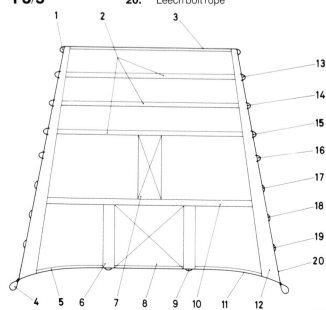

F Spars and rigging

F3/6

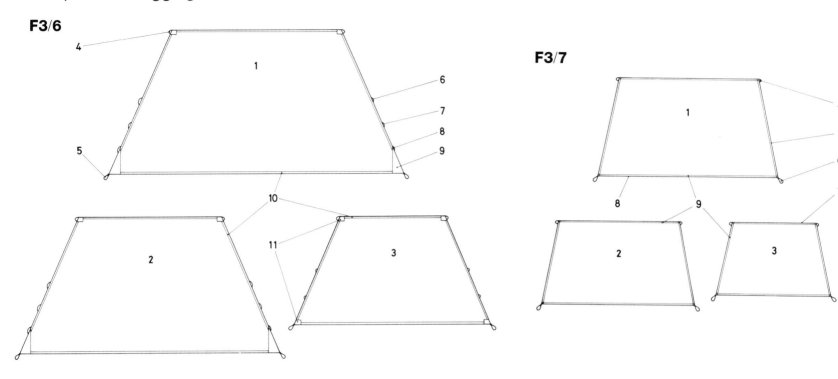

F3/7

F3/8

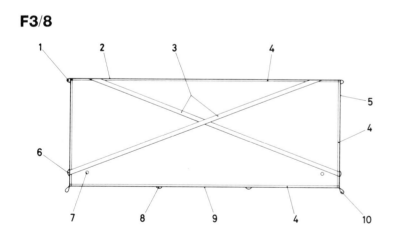

F3/9

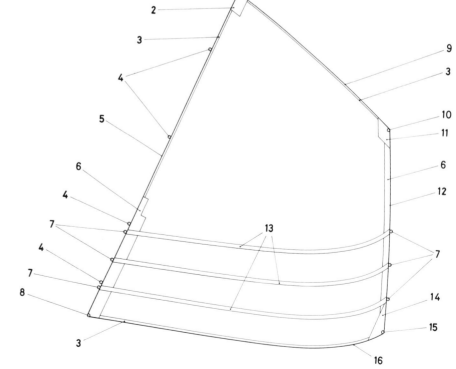

F3/6	**Topgallant sails (1/192 scale)**
1.	Main topgallant sail
2.	Fore topgallant sail
3.	Mizen topgallant sail
4.	Earing
5.	Clew rope
6.	Upper bowline cringle
7.	Middle bowline cringle
8.	Lower bowline cringle
9.	Lining
10.	Tabling
11.	Patches

F3/7	**Royal sails (1/192 scale)**
1.	Main royal sail
2.	Fore royal sail
3.	Mizen royal sail
4.	Earing
5.	Leech bolt rope
6.	Clue rope
7.	Head bolt rope
8.	Foot bolt rope
9.	Tabling

F3/8 Spritsail (1/192 scale)
1. Earing
2. Head bolt rope
3. Reef bands
4. Tabling
5. Leech bolt rope
6. Reef cringle
7. Water hole
8. Bunt line cringle
9. Foot bolt rope
10. Clue rope

F3/9 Driver (1/192 scale)
1. Peak earing thimble
2. Peak piece
3. Tabling
4. Brail thimbles
5. Leech bolt rope
6. Lining
7. Reef thimble
8. Clue thimble
9. Head bolt rope
10. Nock thimble
11. Nock piece
12. Luff bolt rope
13. Reef bands
14. Tack piece
15. Tack thimble
16. Foot bolt rope

F3/10 Mizen staysails (1/192 scale)
1. Mizen staysail
2. Mizen topmast staysail
3. Peak thimble
4. Peak piece
5. Brail cringle
6. Clue piece
7. Clue rope
8. Mizen topgallant staysail
9. Nock thimble
10. Lining
11. Tack thimble

F3/11 Main staysails (1/192 scale)
1. Main staysail
2. Middle staysail
3. Main topgallant staysail
4. Peak thimble
5. Peak piece
6. Clue piece
7. Clue rope
8. Lining
9. Tack thimble
10. Nock thimble

F3/10

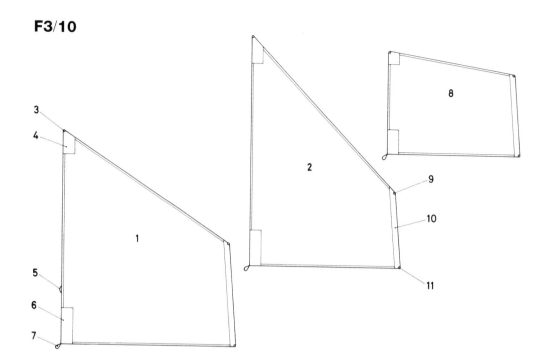

F3/11

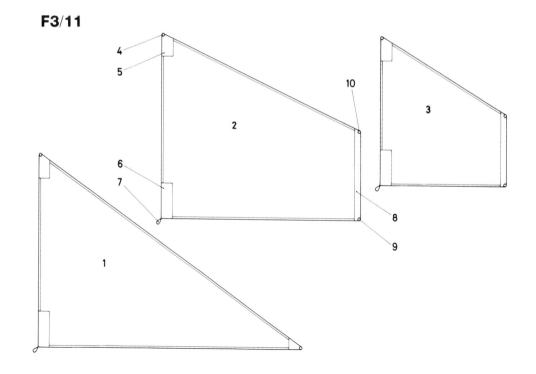

F Spars and rigging

F3/12

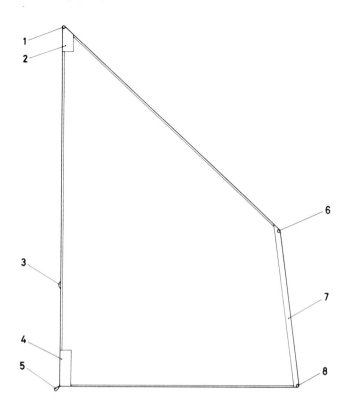

F3/13

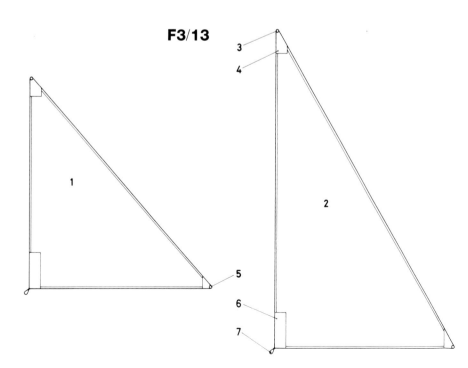

F3/14

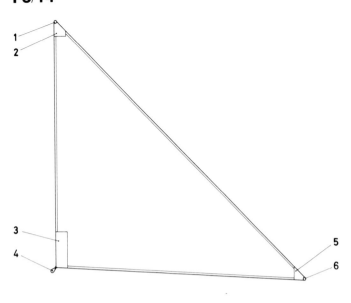

F3/12 Main topmast staysail (1/192 scale)
1. Peak thimble
2. Peak piece
3. Brail cringle
4. Clue piece
5. Clue rope
6. Nock thimble
7. Lining
8. Tack thimble

F3/13 Fore staysails (1/192 scale)
1. Fore staysail
2. Fore topmast staysail
3. Peak thimble
4. Peak piece
5. Tack thimble
6. Clue piece
7. Clue rope

F3/14 Jib (1/192 scale)
1. Peak thimble
2. Peak piece
3. Clue piece
4. Clue rope
5. Lining
6. Tack thimble

F4/1   Halliards (1/384 scale)

1.	Mizen topgallant tye
2.	Mizen topsail tye
3.	Gaff peak halliard
4.	Boom topping lift
5.	Mizen topmast backstay
6.	Traveller on backstay
7.	Mizen topmast halliard
8.	Mizen topgallant halliard
9.	Mizen topgallant yard
10.	Mizen topsail yard
11.	Crossjack sling
12.	Crossjack
13.	Gaff throat halliard
14.	Main topgallant tye
15.	Main topgallant halliard
16.	Main topsail tye
17.	Main topmast backstay
18.	Traveller on backstay
19.	Main topsail halliard
20.	Main topgallant yard
21.	Main topsail yard
22.	Main jeers
23.	Main yard
24.	Fore topgallant tye
25.	Fore topsail tye
26.	Fore topgallant halliard
27.	Fore topmast backstay
28.	Traveller on backstay
29.	Fore topsail halliard
30.	Fore topgallant yard
31.	Fore topsail yard
32.	Fore jeers
33.	Fore yard
34.	Spritsail yard
35.	Spritsail yard halliard

F4/1

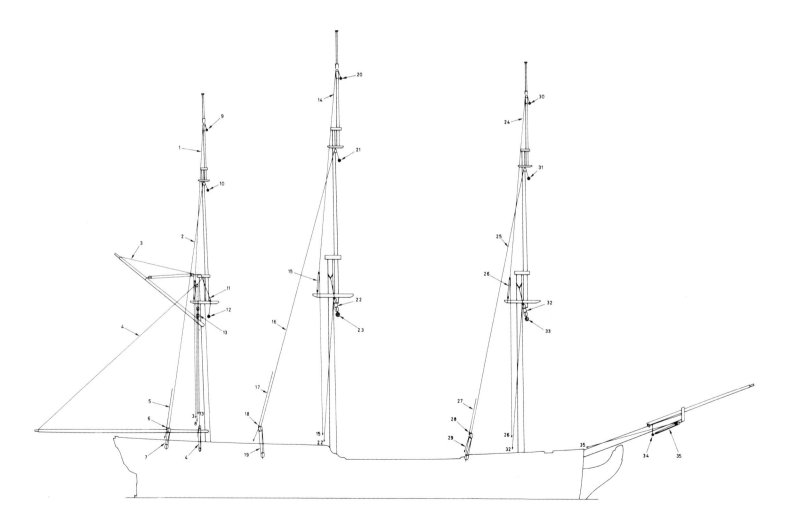

F Spars and rigging

F4/2

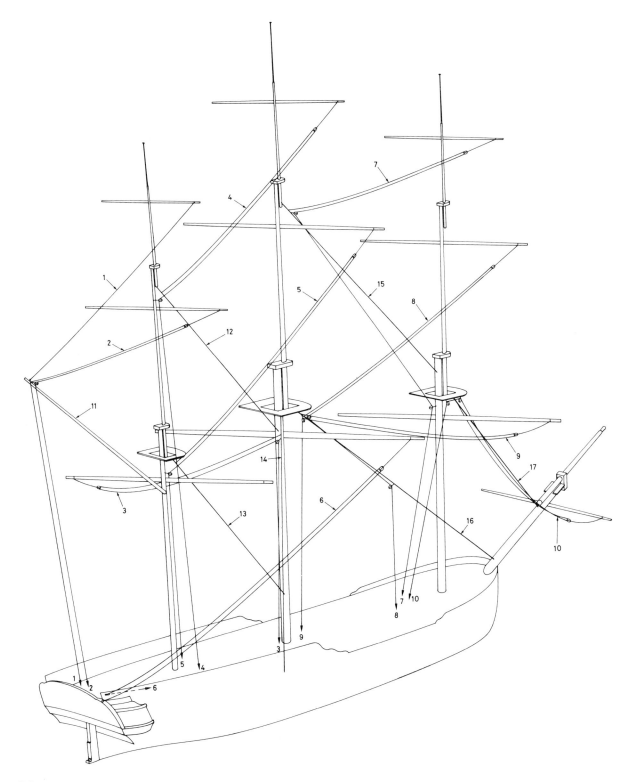

F4/3

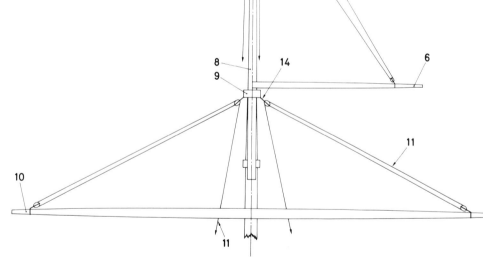

F4/4

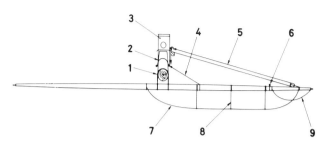

F4/4 Spritsail yard from aft (1/192 scale)

1. Sling
2. Standing lift strap
3. Bowsprit cap
4. Standing lift
5. Lift
6. Jibboom guy pendant thimble
7. Horse
8. Stirrup
9. Flemish horse

F4/5 Driver (no scale)

1. Gaff
2. Vang pendants
3. Vang purchases
4. Boom
5. Guy pendants
6. Guy purchases
7. Boom sheet

F4/5

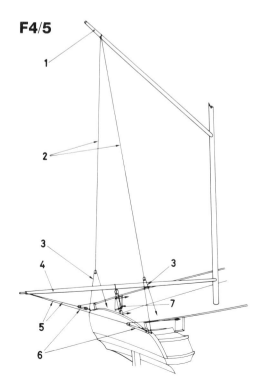

F4/3 Main yard lifts from forward (larboard side – yards hoisted; starboard side – yards lowered; 1/192 scale)

1. Common pole head	7. Topsail lift
2. Topgallant yard	8. Topmast
3. Topgallant lift	9. Lower mast cap
4. Topgallant mast	10. Lower yard
5. Topmast cap	11. Main lift
6. Topsail yard	12. Thimble seized between the two foremast topgallant shrouds
	13. Sister block seized between the two foremost topmast shrouds
	14. Span

F Spars and rigging

F4/6 Lower yard – sling and truss (no scale)

1. Lower mast cap
2. Nave line
3. Top
4. Lower yard
5. Truss pendant
6. Bolster
7. Sling
8. Laniard
9. Strap
10. Sling cleats

F4/6

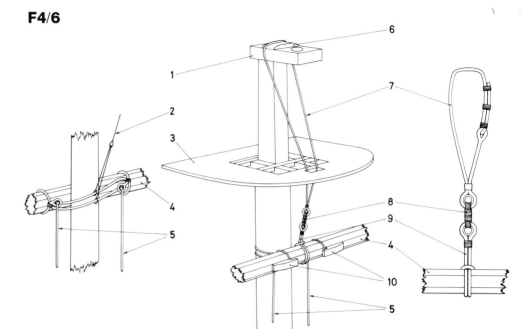

F4/7

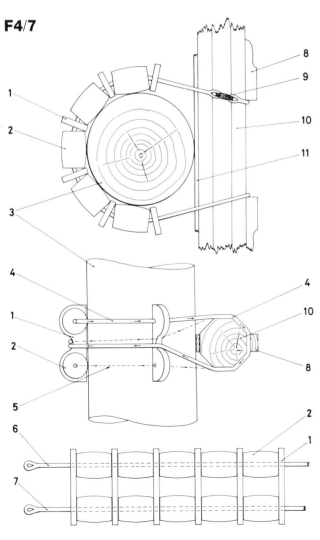

F4/7 Topsail yard – parral (1/24 scale)

1. Rib
2. Truck
3. Topmast
4. Upper parral rope
5. Line of lower parral rope
6. Upper parral rope with parral unrigged
7. Lower parral rope
8. Cleat
9. Spunyarn seizing
10. Topsail yard
11. Batten

F5 RUNNING RIGGING – SAILS

F5/1 Main course (fore side on the left; after side on the right; 1/192 scale)

1. Yard tackle pendant
2. Brace pendant
3. Bowline bridles
4. Bowline
5. Yardarm cleat
6. Futtock shroud
7. Main top
8. Leech line
9. Bunt lines
10. Quarter block
11. Main shroud
12. Inner tricing line
13. Yard tackle triced up
14. Outer tricing line
15. Horse
16. Stirrup
17. Yard tackle pendant triced up
18. Topsail sheet block
19. Slabline
20. Clew garnet
21. Sheet block
22. Tack

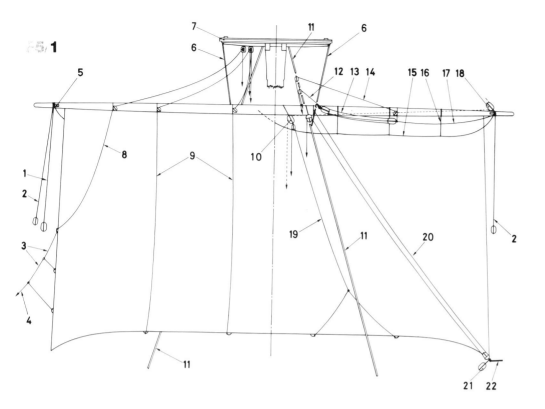

F-5/**1**

F5/2 **Main topsail (fore side on the left; after side on the right; 1/192 scale)**

F5/2 **Main topsail (fore side on the left; after side on the right; 1/192 scale)**
1. Topsail yard
2. Brace pendant
3. Bowline bridles
4. Bowline
5. Lower yard
6. Bunt line
7. Topsail tye block
8. Topmast cross tree
9. Sister block seized between the two foremost shrouds
10. Reef tackle pendant
11. Stirrup
12. Topgallant sheet
13. Yardarm sheave
14. Reef tackle
15. Topmast shroud
16. Horse
17. Clew line
18. Futtock shroud
19. Topsail sheet
20. Flemish horse

F5/3 **Main topgallant sail (fore side on the left; after side on the right; 1/192 scale)**
1. Topgallant yard
2. Bowline bridle
3. Toggled bowline
4. Horse
5. Clue line
6. Topsail yard
7. Sheet

F5/2

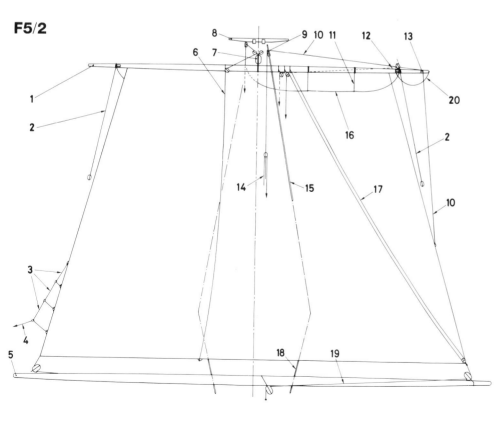

F5/3

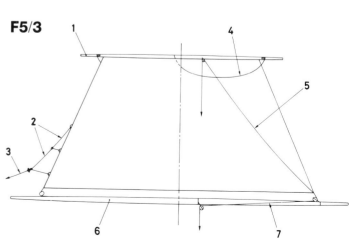

97

F5/4

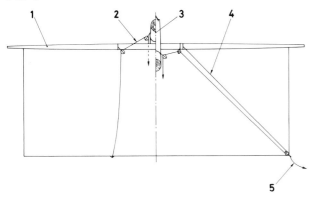

F5/5

F5/4   Spritsail (fore side on the left; after side on the right; 1/192 scale)

1. Spritsail yard
2. Bunt line
3. Bowsprit
4. Clue line
5. Sheet

F5/5   Driver (1/192 scale)

1. Ensign halliard
2. Peak brail
3. Middle brail
4. Throat brail
5. Foot brail
6. Sheet
7. Gaff
8. Mizen mast
9. Parral
10. Saddle
11. Horse
12. Comb cleat
13. Boom
14. Sheet cleat
15. Mast hoops

F5/6   Mizen staysails (1/192 scale)

1. Mizen topgallant staysail
2. Mizen topgallant stay
3. Mizen topgallant staysail halliard
4. Mizen topgallant staysail downhauler
5. Mizen topgallant staysail sheet (double)
6. Mizen topgallant staysail tack (double)
7. Main topmast shroud
8. Mizen topmast staysail
9. Mizen topmast stay
10. Mizen topmast staysail halliard
11. Mizen topmast staysail downhauler
12. Mizen topmast staysail sheet (double)
13. Mizen topmast staysail tack (double)
14. Main shroud
15. Mizen staysail
16. Mizen staysail stay
17. Mizen staysail halliard
18. Mizen staysail downhauler
19. Mizen staysail sheet
20. Mizen staysail tack
21. Mizen staysail brail
22. Mizen shroud
23. Mizen mast
24. Main mast

F5/7   Main staysails (1/192 scale)

1. Main mast
2. Main topgallant staysail
3. Main topgallant staysail stay
4. Main topgallant staysail halliard
5. Main topgallant staysail downhauler
6. Main topgallant staysail sheet (double)
7. Main topgallant staysail tack (double)
8. Fore topmast shroud
9. Middle staysail
10. Middle staysail stay (starboard)
11. Middle staysail halliard (starboard)
12. Middle staysail downhauler
13. Middle staysail sheet (double)
14. Middle staysail tack (double)
15. Main topmast staysail
16. Main topmast preventer stay
17. Main topmast staysail halliard (larboard)
18. Main topmast staysail downhauler
19. Main topmast staysail sheet (double)
20. Main topmast staysail tack (double)
21. Main topmast staysail brail
22. Fore mast
23. Fore shroud
24. Main staysail
25. Main staysail stay
26. Main staysail halliard
27. Main staysail downhauler
28. Main staysail sheet (double)
29. Main staysail tack
30. Main bowline block
31. Middle staysail stay tricing line

F5/6

F5/7

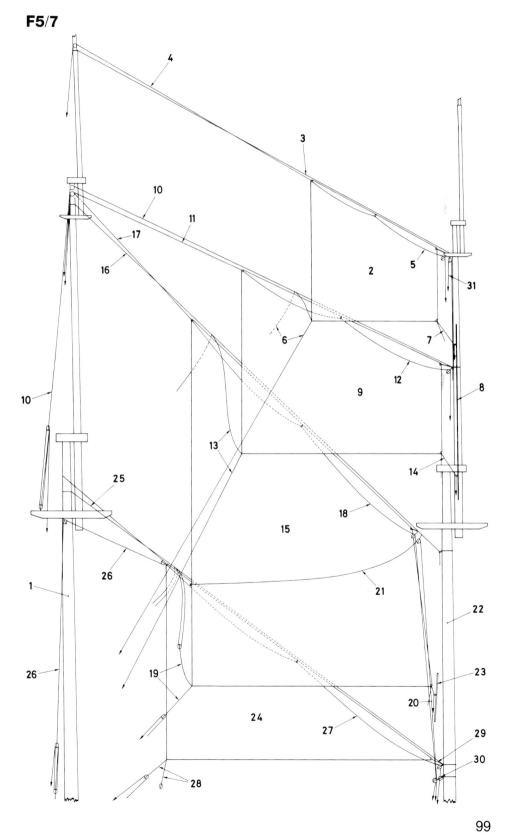

F5/8

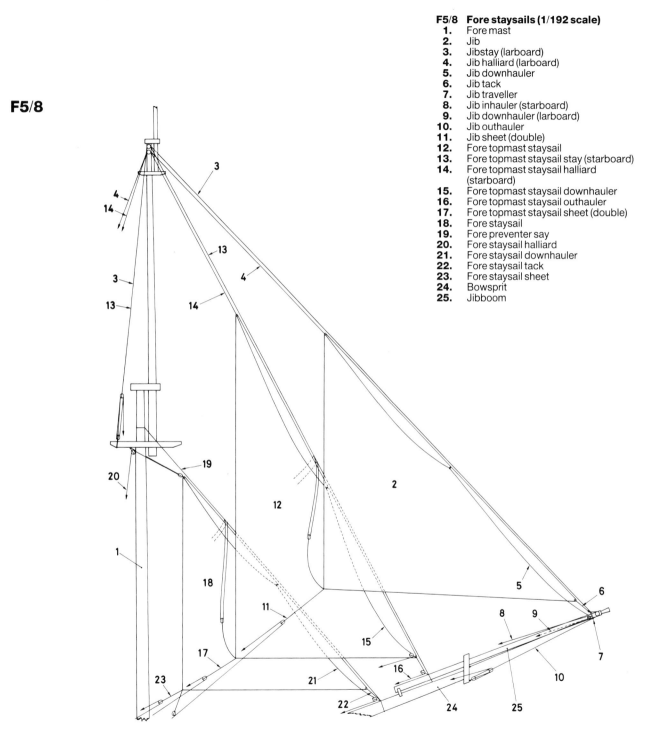

F5/8 Fore staysails (1/192 scale)
1. Fore mast
2. Jib
3. Jibstay (larboard)
4. Jib halliard (larboard)
5. Jib downhauler
6. Jib tack
7. Jib traveller
8. Jib inhauler (starboard)
9. Jib downhauler (larboard)
10. Jib outhauler
11. Jib sheet (double)
12. Fore topmast staysail
13. Fore topmast staysail stay (starboard)
14. Fore topmast staysail halliard (starboard)
15. Fore topmast staysail downhauler
16. Fore topmast staysail outhauler
17. Fore topmast staysail sheet (double)
18. Fore staysail
19. Fore preventer say
20. Fore staysail halliard
21. Fore staysail downhauler
22. Fore staysail tack
23. Fore staysail sheet
24. Bowsprit
25. Jibboom

F5/9

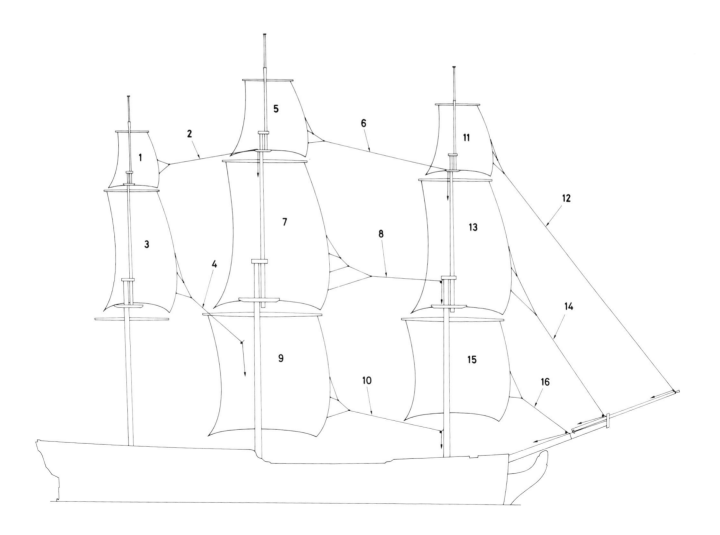

F Spars and rigging

F5/10 Belaying plan (1/192 scale)

F5/11 Belaying profile (1/192 scale)

F5/12 Belaying locations (1/96 scale)
A. Taffarel
B. Mizen topsail sheet bitts
C. Mizen mast
D. Fore brace bitts
E. Quarterdeck breast rail
F. Main mast
G. After skid beams
H. Main jeer bitts
I. Main topsail sheet bitts
J. Forward skid beams
K. Forecastle breast beam
L. Belfry
M. Fore jeer bitts
N. Fore mast
O. Fore topsail sheet bitts
P. Breasthook pin rail

Crossjack
1. Truss pendant
2. Nave line
3. Braces (starboard brace belays on larboard side and vice versa)
4. Lifts

Main course
5. Truss pendants
6. Nave line
7. Jeers
8. Outer tricing lines
9. Inner tricing lines
10. Braces

11. Lifts
12. Leech lines
13. Bunt lines
14. Clue garnets
15. Sheets
16. Tacks
17. Bowlines
18. Slablines

Fore course
19. Truss pendants
20. Nave line
21. Jeers
22. Outer tricing lines
23. Inner tricing lines
24. Braces
25. Lifts
26. Leech lines
27. Bunt lines
28. Clue garnets
29. Sheets
30. Tacks
31. Bowlines
32. Slablines

Mizen topsail
33. Lifts
34. Halliard
35. Braces
36. Clue lines
37. Reef tackles
38. Bunt lines
39. Bowlines (starboard bowline belays on larboard side and vice versa)
40. Sheets

Main topsail
41. Lifts
42. Halliards
43. Braces
44. Clue lines
45. Reef tackles
46. Bunt lines
47. Bowlines
48. Sheets

Fore topsail
49. Lifts
50. Halliards
51. Braces
52. Clue lines
53. Reef tackles
54. Bunt lines
55. Bowlines
56. Sheets

Mizen topgallant sail
57. Lifts
58. Halliards
59. Braces
60. Clue lines
61. Bowlines
62. Sheets

Main topgallant sail
63. Lifts
64. Halliards (main top)
65. Braces
66. Clue lines
67. Bowlines
68. Sheets

F5/10

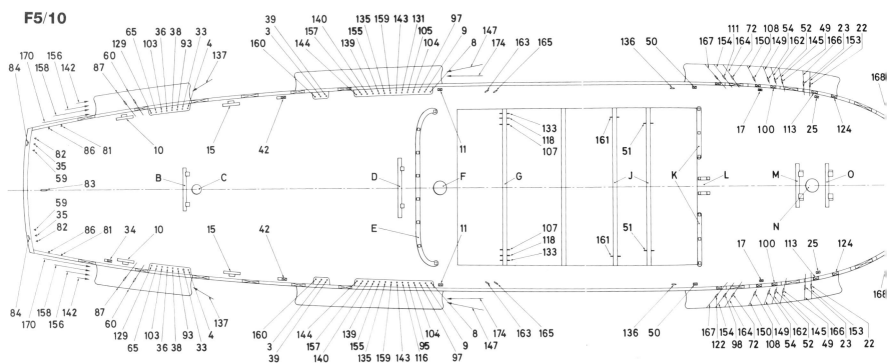

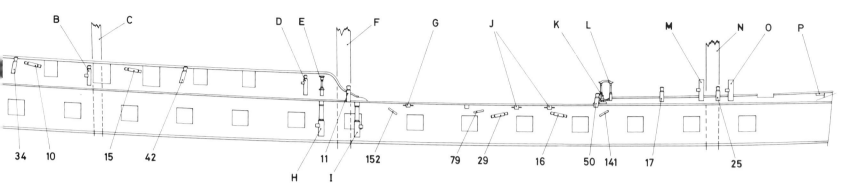

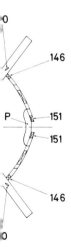

Fore topgallant sail
69. Lifts (fore top)
70. Halliards
71. Braces
72. Clue lines
73. Bowlines
74. Sheets

Spritsail
75. Braces
76. Lifts
77. Bunt lines
78. Clue lines
79. Sheets

Driver
80. Throat halliard
81. Peak halliard
82. Vangs
83. Boom sheet
84. Guys
85. Topping lifts
86. Peak brails
87. Middle brails
88. Throat brails
89. Foot brails
90. Sheet

Mizen staysail
91. Halliard
92. Downhauler
93. Sheets
94. Brails

Main staysail
95. Halliard
96. Downhauler
97. Sheets

Fore staysail
98. Halliard
99. Downhauler
100. Sheets

Mizen topmast staysail
101. Halliard
102. Downhauler
103. Sheets
104. Tacks

Main topmast staysail
105. Halliard
106. Downhauler
107. Sheets
108. Tacks
109. Brails

Fore topmast staysail
110. Stay
111. Halliard
112. Downhauler
113. Sheets
114. Outhauler

Middle staysail
115. Stay
116. Halliard
117. Downhauler
118. Sheets
119. Tacks (fore top)
120. Tricing line (fore top)

Jib
121. Stay
122. Halliard
123. Downhauler
124. Sheets
125. Inhauler
126. Outhauler

Mizen topgallant staysail
127. Halliard
128. Downhauler (main top)
129. Sheets
130. Tacks (main top)

Main topgallant staysail
131. Halliard
132. Downhauler (fore top)
133. Sheets
134. Tacks (fore top)

Main studding sail
135. Topping lift
136. Fore guy
137. After guy
138. Martingale
139. Outer halliard
140. Inner halliard

141. Fore tack
142. After tack
143. Fore sheet
144. After sheet

Fore studding sail
145. Topping lift
146. Fore guy
147. After guy
148. Martingale
149. Outer halliard
150. Inner halliard
151. Fore tack
152. After tack
153. Fore sheet
154. After sheet

Main topmast studding sail
155. Topping lift
156. Brace
157. Halliard
158. Tack
159. Fore sheet
160. After sheet
161. Downhauler

Fore topmast studding sail
162. Topping lift
163. Brace
164. Halliard
165. Tack
166. Fore sheet
167. After sheet
168. Downhauler

Main topgallant studding sail
169. Halliard (main top)
170. Tack
171. Fore sheet (main topsail yard)
172. After sheet (main top)

Fore topgallant studding sail
173. Halliard (fore top)
174. Tack
175. Fore sheet (fore topsail yard)
176. After sheet (fore top)

F5/12

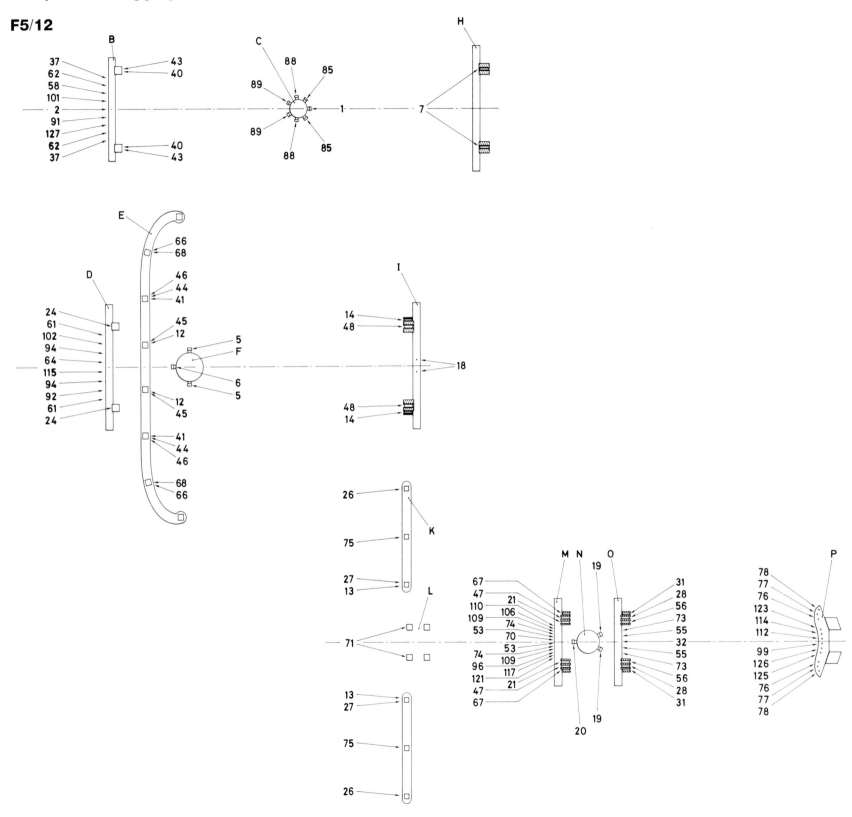

F6 STUDDING SAILS

F6/1 Main mast booms run out, from aft (1/384 scale)
1. Topgallant yard
2. Topsail yard
3. Lower yard
4. Topgallant studding sail boom
5. Topmast studding sail boom
6. Boom running-out tackle
7. Topping lift pendant
8. Brace
9. Lower boom
10. Topping lift
11. Fore guy
12. After guy
13. Martingale

F6/2 Main mast studding sails rigged, from aft (1/384 scale)
1. Topgallant sail
2. Topgallant studding sail
3. Topgallant studding sail halliard
4. Topgallant studding sail tack
5. Topgallant studding sail sheet
6. Topsail
7. Topmast studding sail
8. Topmast studding sail halliard
9. Topmast studding sail tack
10. Topmast studding sail forward sheet
11. Topmast studding sail after sheet
12. Topmast studding sail downhauler
13. Course
14. Lower studding sail
15. Lower studding sail outer halliard
16. Lower studding sail inner halliard
17. Lower studding sail forward tack
18. Lower studding sail after tack
19. Lower studding sail forward sheet
20. Lower studding sail after sheet

F6/3 Main mast studding sails (1/192 scale)
1. Lower studding sail
2. Topmast studding sail
3. Topgallant studding sail
4. Reef bands
5. Earing cringles
6. Reef earing cringles
7. Downhauler cringle
8. Clew cringles
9. Tabling
10. Bolt rope
11. Piece

F6/3

F6/1

F6/2

G1/1

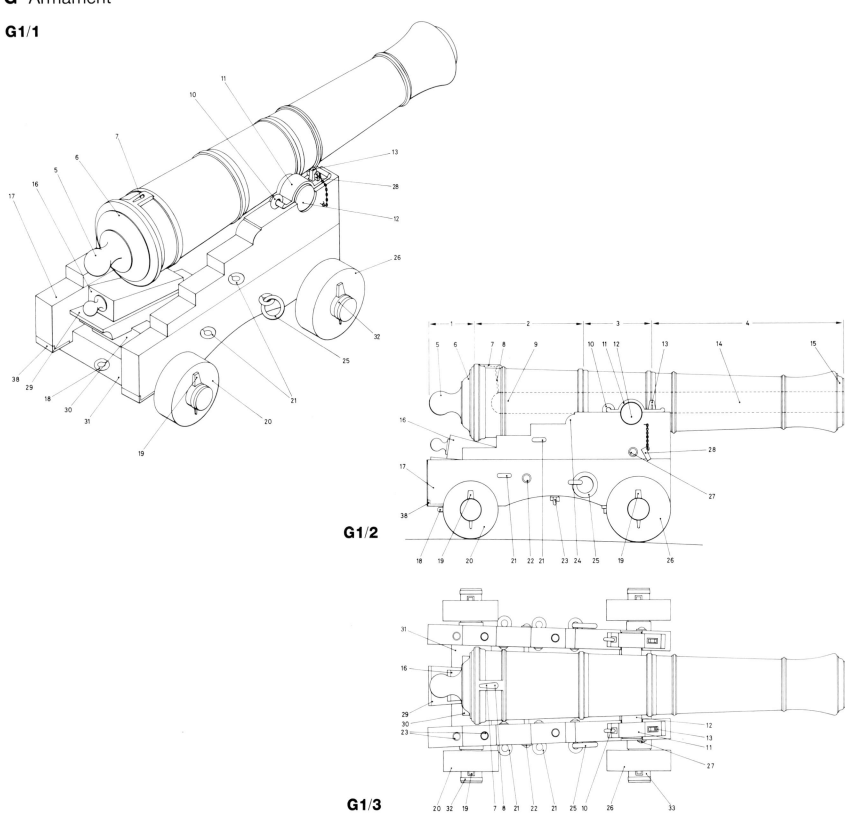

G1/2

G1/3

G1/4

G1/5

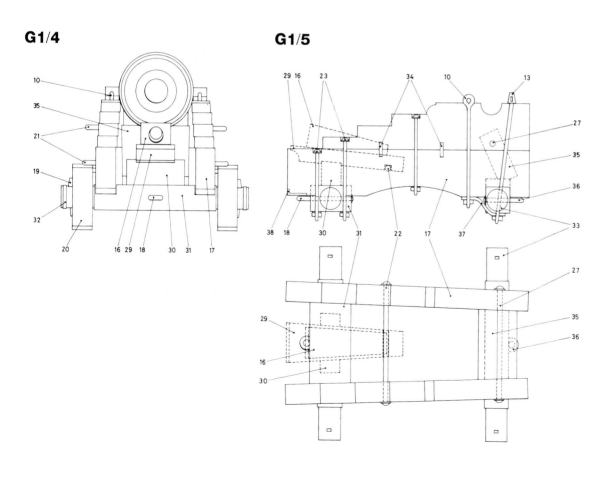

G Armament

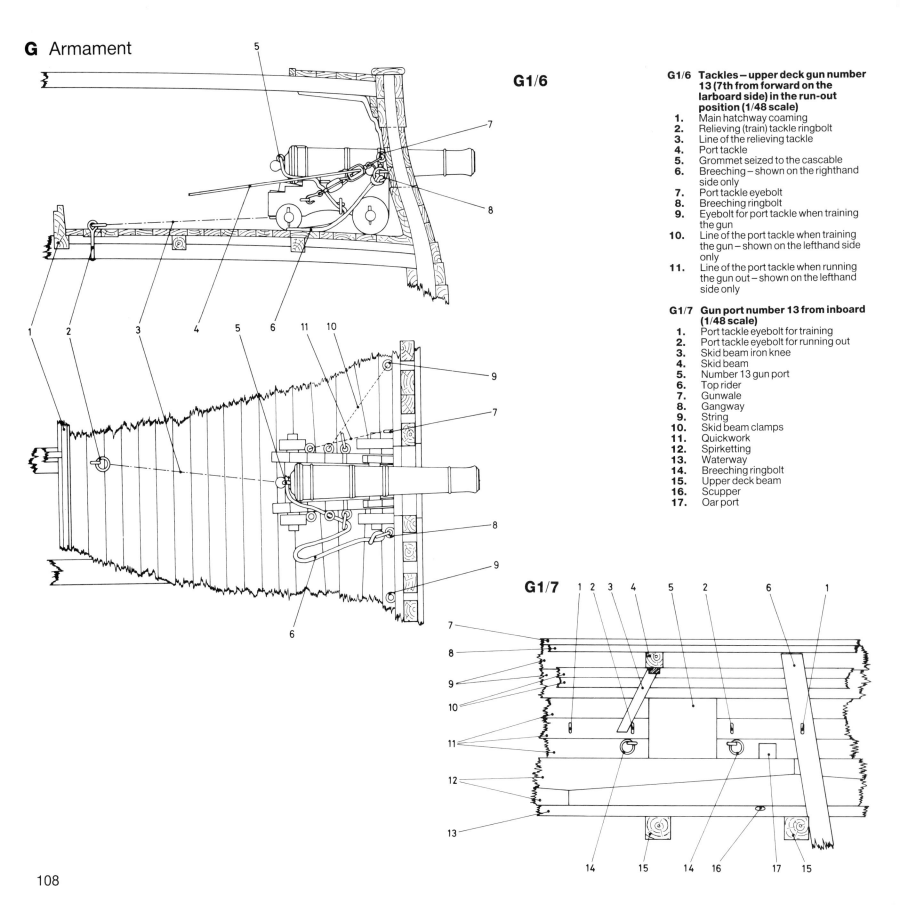

G1/6

G1/7

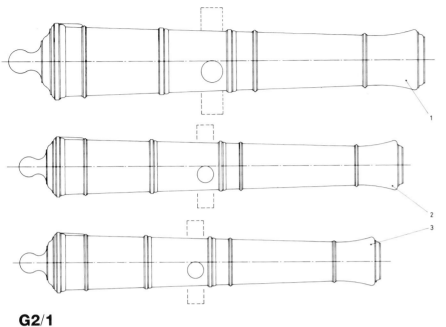

G2/1

G2   9-POUNDER 7-FOOT AND 7-FOOT 6-INCH CARRIAGE GUNS

G2/1   Size comparisons (1/24 scale)
1. 18-pounder 8-foot – upper deck
2. 9-pounder 7-foot 6-inch – forecastle chase
3. 9-pounder 7-foot – quarterdeck

G3   32-POUNDER CARRONADE (all 1/24 scale)

G3/1   Side elevation
1. Elevating screw box
2. Cascable ring (breeching loop)
3. Joint bolt
4. Step sight
5. Elevating screw
6. Eyebolt for port tackle
7. Socket for iron crow
8. Truck
9. Bolt
10. Eyebolt for training tackle
11. Skead or slide
12. Breeching ringbolt
13. Carriage
14. Joint chocks
15. Gudgeon
16. Fighting bolt

G3/2   Front elevation
1. Step sight
2. Cascable loop
3. Joint bolt
4. Breeching ringbolt
5. Fighting bolt
6. Joint chock
7. Carriage
8. Skead or slide

G3/1

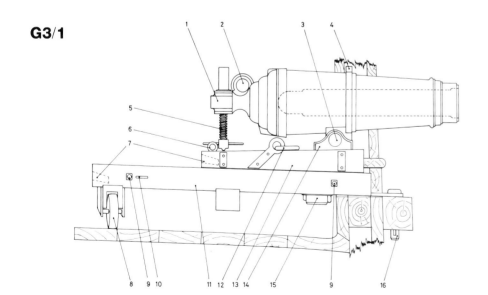

G3/2

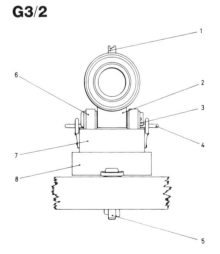

G Armament

G3/3

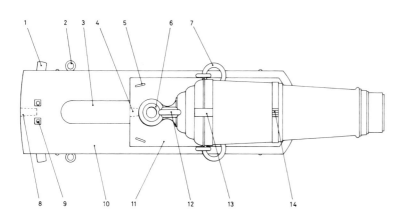

G3/3 Plan
1. Truck
2. Eyebolt for training tackle
3. Slot for gudgeon
4. Socket for iron crow
5. Eyebolt for port tackle
6. Elevating screw box
7. Breeching ringbolt
8. Socket for iron crow
9. Bolt
10. Skead or slide
11. Carriage
12. Cascable ring
13. Base patch
14. Step sight

G3/4

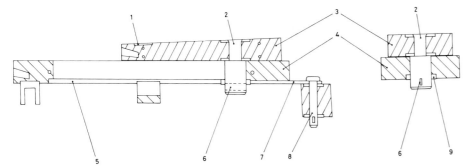

G3/4 Longitudinal section of carriage and skead on centre line with transverse section through gudgeon
1. Elevating screw plate
2. Gudgeon
3. Carriage
4. Skead or slide
5. Slot for gudgeon ring
6. Forelock slot
7. Iron plate bracket for fighting bolt
8. Fighting bolt
9. Gudgeon ring

G3/5 Skead from below and rear elevation of carriage and skead
1. Slot for gudgeon
2. Gudgeon
3. Iron plate bracket for fighting bolt
3. Truck
4. Eyebolt for training tackle
6. Socket for iron crow
7. Carriage
8. Skead or slide
9. Iron plate bracket

G3/5

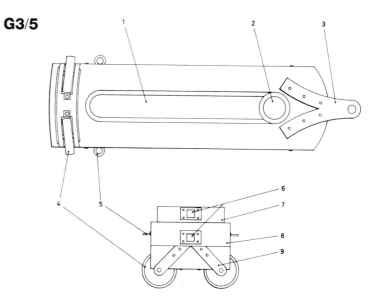

G3/6

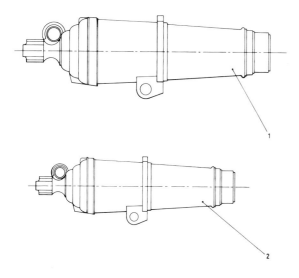

G4/1

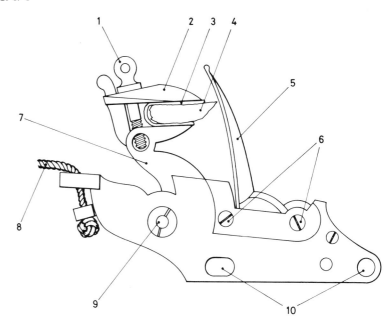

G3/6 Size comparisons
1. 32-pounder as fitted in 1795
2. 18-pounder as fitted temporarily in 1794

G4 GUN EQUIPMENT

G4/1 Gun lock (½ scale)
1. Cock screw
2. Jaw
3. Leather
4. Flint
5. Hammer
6. Plate pins
7. Cock
8. Lanyard
9. Pin and nut
10. Fixing holes

G4/2 Gun tools (1/24 scale)
1. Rope sponge with rammer head
2. Sponge
3. Rammer
4. Wad hook

G4/2

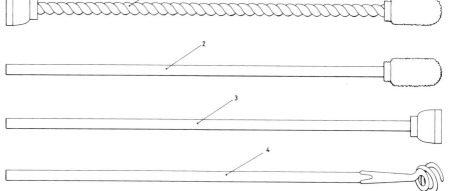

111

H1/1

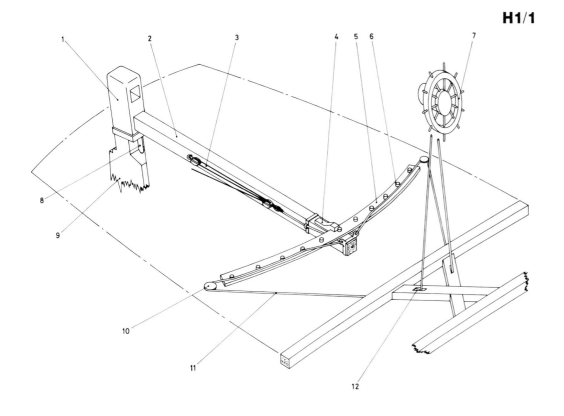

H1 WHEEL AND TILLER

H1/1 Schematic (no scale)
1. Rudder head
2. Tiller
3. Tensioning tackle
4. Gooseneck
5. Sweep
6. Roller
7. Wheel
8. Upper pintle
9. Rudder
10. Horizontal sheave
11. Tiller rope
12. Vertical sheave

H1/2 Arrangement – elevation (lower hance in original designed position, not as built; 1/96 scale)
1. Counter timber
2. Quarterdeck
3. Mizen mast
4. Wheel
5. Rudder
6. Stern post
7. Upper deck
8. Tiller
9. Gooseneck
10. Sweep
11. Tiller rope

H1/3 Arrangement – plan (1/96 scale)
1. Rudder head
2. Tiller
3. Gooseneck
4. Sweep
5. Mizen mast
6. Vertical sheave
7. Horizontal sheave
8. Tiller rope

H1/2

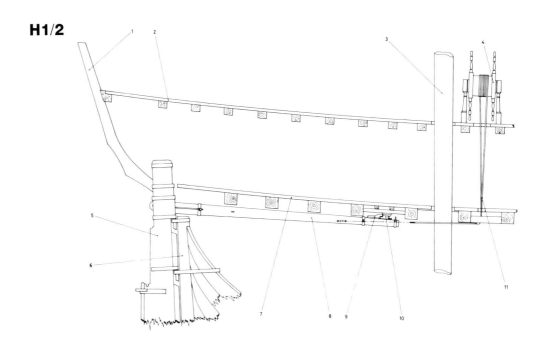

H1/3

H2/1

H2   WHEEL

H2/1 Arrangement (1/24 scale)
1. Spoke
2. Felloe
3. Stanchion
4. Knave
5. Drum
6. Handle

H2/2 Construction (1/24 scale)
1. Handle
2. Felloe
3. Spoke
4. Knave
5. Spindle
6. Drum

H2/2

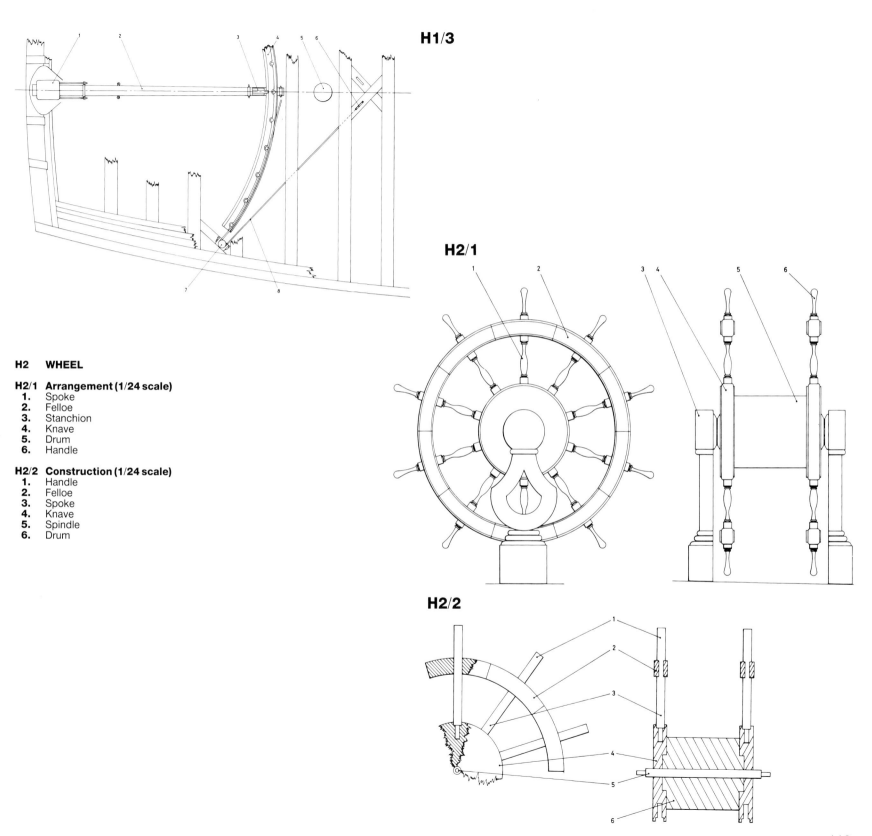

H3/1

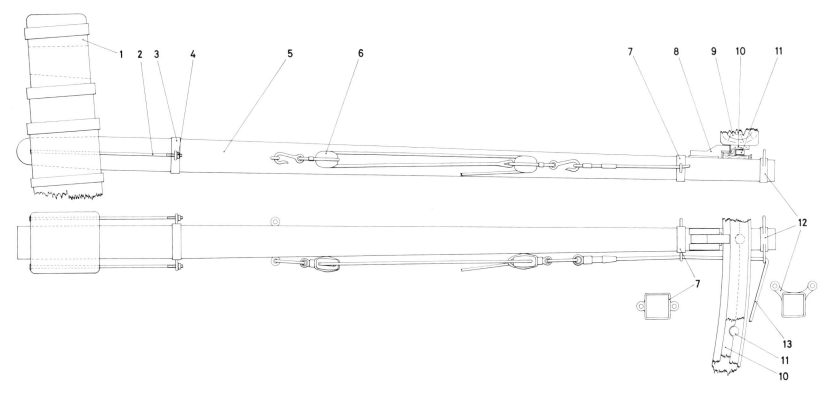

H3/2

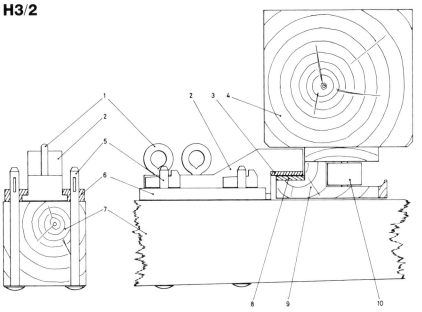

H3   TILLER AND SWEEP

H3/1   Arrangement (1/32 scale)
1.   Rudder head
2.   Tiller securing bolt
3.   Eye hoop for tiller securing bolt
4.   Tightening nut
5.   Tiller
6.   Tensioning tackle
7.   Eye hoop
8.   Shifting gooseneck
9.   Upper deck beam
10.   Sweep
11.   Roller
12.   Horn hoop
13.   Tiller rope

H3/2   Shifting gooseneck (1/8 scale)
1.   Screw cut eyebolt
2.   Shifting gooseneck
3.   Brass plate on shifting gooseneck
4.   Upper deck beam
5.   Forelocked bolts
6.   Fixed slide
7.   Tiller
8.   Iron plate on sweep
9.   Sweep
10.   Lignum vitae roller

H4   RUDDER

H4/1   Arrangement (1/48 scale)
1.   Head hoops
2.   Upper pintle strap
3.   Upper hance
4.   Hook for rudder pendant chain
5.   Lower hance
6.   Ring plate
7.   Pintle strap
8.   Back piece
9.   Sole
10.   Inner post
11.   Hole for spare tiller
12.   Hole for tiller
13.   Stern post
14.   Score
15.   Brace strap
16.   Pintle
17.   Bearding
18.   Keel
19.   False keel

H4/2   Construction (1/48 scale)
1.   Two-part main piece (oak)
2.   Back piece (fir)
3.   Fir piece
4.   Sole (fir)
5.   Section through head
6.   Section between hances
7.   Section through rudder
8.   Bearding piece (elm)

H4/1

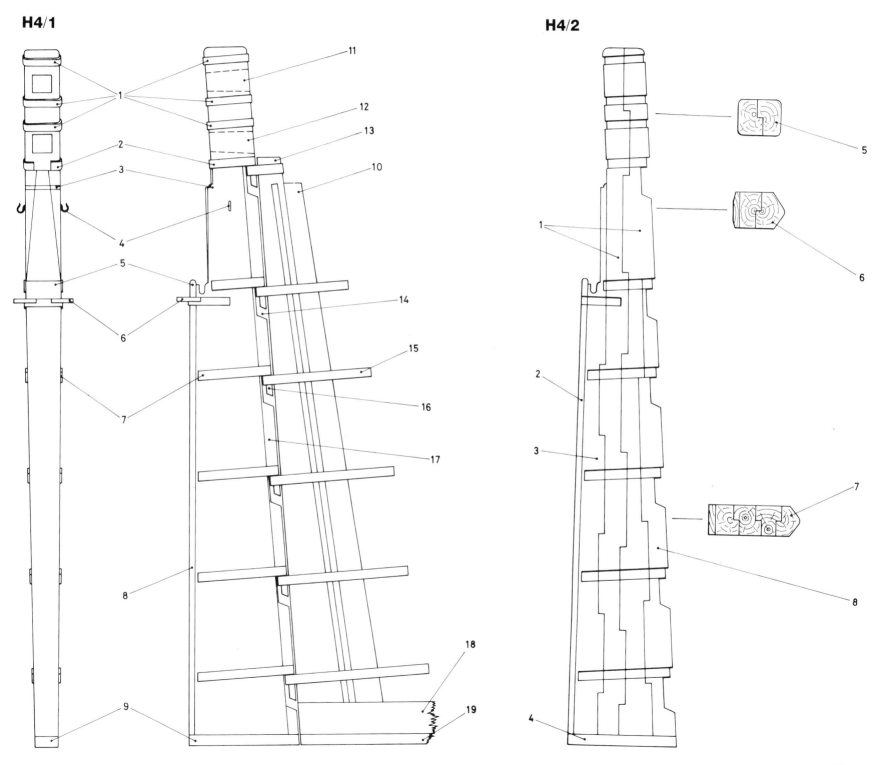

H4/2

H Helm

H4/3

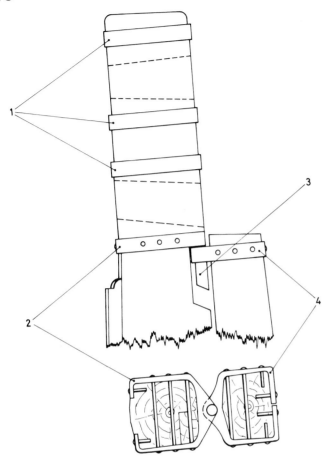

H4/3 Upper irons (1/24 scale)
1. Head hoops
2. Upper pintle strap
3. Upper pintle
4. Upper brace

H4/4 Lower hance irons and ring plate (1/24 scale)
1. Back piece
2. Ring plate
3. Main piece
4. Pintle strap
5. Pintle
6. Brace
7. Stern post
8. Outer hull planking

H4/4

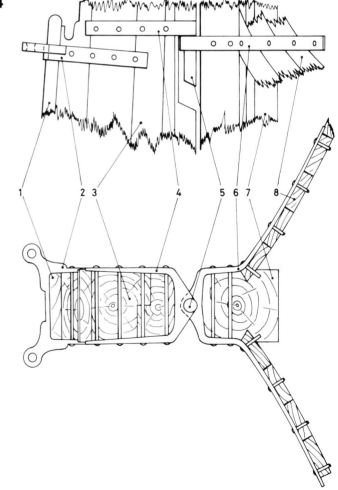

I Boats

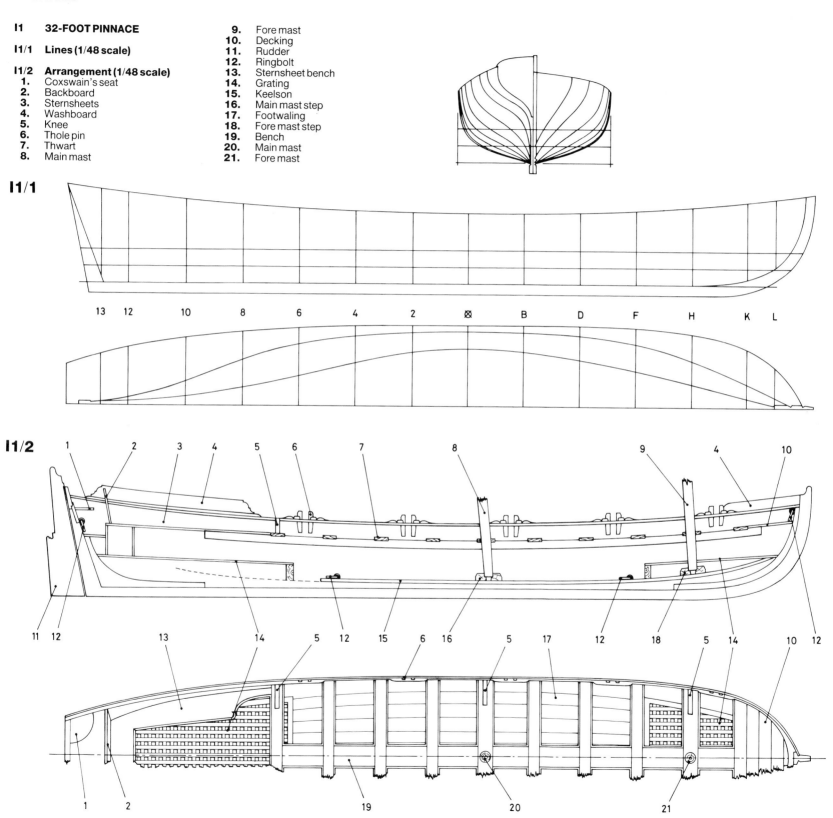

I1/1

13   12   10   8   6   4   2   ⊗   B   D   F   H   K   L

I1/2

1   2   3   4   5   6   7   8   9   4   10

11   12   14   5   12   15   6   16   12   18   5   14   10   12

13   14   5   6   5   17   5   14   10

1   2   19   20   21

I Boats

I2/1

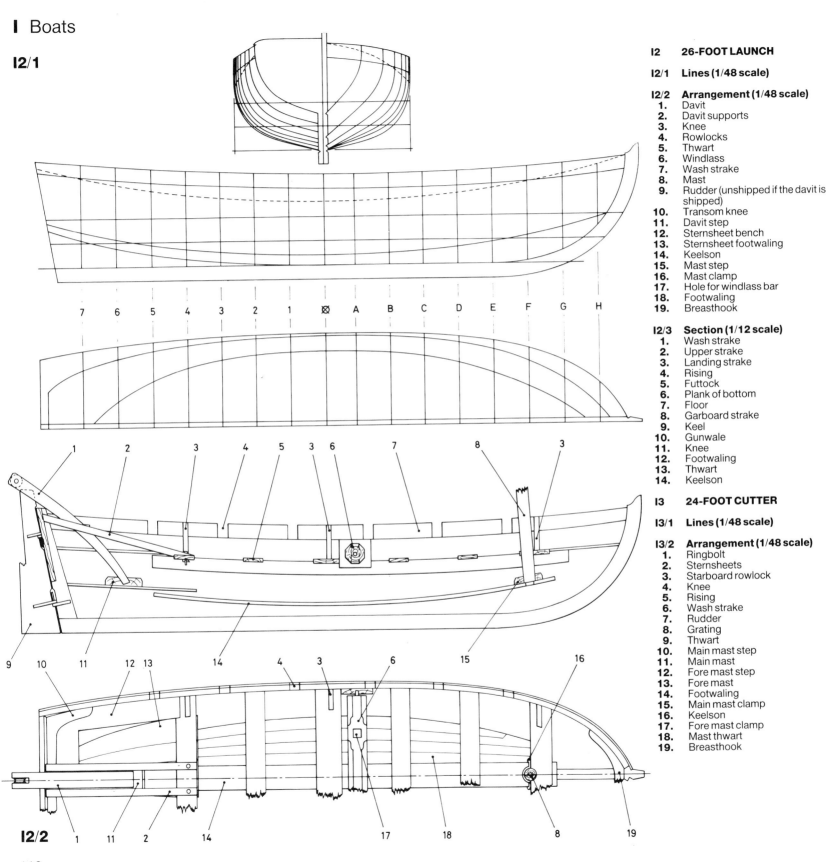

7 6 5 4 3 2 1 ⊗ A B C D E F G H

I2/2

1 11 2 14 3 6 18 8 19